FUNDAMENTALS OF

Reference

ALA FUNDAMENTALS SERIES

FUNDAMENTALS OF

Reference

CAROLYN M. MULAC

ALA FUNDAMENTALS SERIES

American Library Association : Chicago   2012

Carolyn M. Mulac has more than thirty years' experience in reference work. An active member of ALA's Reference and User Services Association (RUSA), she has served on a number of committees and chaired the *Reference Books Bulletin* Editorial Board, the Dartmouth Medal Committee, and the Management of Reference Committee. She has reviewed reference sources for *Booklist* since 1991 and contributed to the 6th and 7th editions of *Reference Sources for Small and Medium-Sized Libraries*. She also reviews books on the performing arts for *Library Journal* and contributes to *Booklist's* Points of Reference blog. In 2008 she received the Illinois Library Association's Reference Services Award.

© 2012 by the American Library Association. Any claim of copyright is subject to applicable limitations and exceptions, such as rights of fair use and library copying pursuant to Sections 107 and 108 of the U.S. Copyright Act. No copyright is claimed for content in the public domain, such as works of the U.S. government.

Printed in the United States of America

16 15 14 13 12   5 4 3 2 1

Extensive effort has gone into ensuring the reliability of the information in this book; however, the publisher makes no warranty, express or implied, with respect to the material contained herein.

ISBNs: 978-0-8389-1087-0 (paper); 978-0-8389-9489-4 (PDF); 978-0-8389-9490-0 (ePub); 978-0-8389-9491-7 (Kindle). For more information on digital formats, visit the ALA Store at alastore.ala.org and select eEditions.

Library of Congress Cataloging-in-Publication Data
Mulac, Carolyn.
  Fundamentals of reference / Carolyn Mulac.
     pages   cm. — (ALA fundamentals series)
  Includes bibliographical references and indexes.
  ISBN 978-0-8389-1087-0 (pbk. : alk. paper) 1. Reference services (Libraries)—United States. 2. Reference sources—Bibliography. 3. Internet in library reference services. I. Title.
  Z711.M82 2012
  025.5'20973—dc23
                                                          2012010058

Book design by Casey Bayer in Eau Douce and Berkeley.
Cover image © photobank.ch/Shutterstock, Inc.

♾ This paper meets the requirements of ANSI/NISO Z39.48-1992 (Permanence of Paper).

To the memory of my parents, Joseph A. and Dorothy A. Mulac.

Dad, you often told me I should write a book . . .

CONTENTS

ACKNOWLEDGMENTS

R EFERENCE WORK IS not a solitary pursuit and neither is writing a book about it. I'd like to thank Jack O'Gorman, Peggy A. Sullivan, and Dave Tyckoson for their encouragement; Jelena Radicevic and Greta M. Bever for their support; Linda Ward-Callaghan, Carolyn A. Sheehy, and Rosemary C. Wojdyla for their wisdom and friendship; and my family for their love and especially their patience.

ACKNOWLEDGEMENTS

INTRODUCTION

R EFERENCE LIBRARIANS KNOW a little about a lot of things. Our work is a mosaic of subjects, formats, and modes of service, and we are constantly adding pieces of information, bits of experience, and shards of knowledge. The purpose of *Fundamentals of Reference* is to present an outline of the big picture that is reference. Further reading, study, and experience will fill in the details and create the reader's own reference mosaic.

Fundamentals of Reference is intended as an introduction to reference sources and services for a variety of readers, from library staff members who are asked to work in a reference department for a short period of time to managers and other librarians who wish to familiarize themselves with this area of the profession. Students in graduate programs of library and information science (LIS) and library technical assistant programs may also find it helpful.

In part 1, which covers reference sources, the print and electronic tools of the reference trade are discussed. In part 2, the focus is on various types of reference service, including telephone and electronic reference, as well as reference evaluation, policies, and standards.

The bibliography includes a variety of readings about reference, and the appendix features a number of key American Library Association (ALA) documents.

Fundamentals of Reference is my look at the tools and techniques of reference through the lens of more than thirty years as a reference librarian. The views expressed and mistakes made are entirely my own.

PART 1

Reference Sources

Knowledge is of two kinds. We know a subject ourselves,
or we know where we can find information upon it.

—Samuel Johnson

R EFERENCE LIBRARIANS, TOO, are of at least two kinds: subject specialists whose expertise consists of an in-depth knowledge of a single subject or related subjects in a single field, and generalists, who are familiar with the main ideas of a variety of topics. I count myself among the latter.

A popular conception of reference librarians might have us spouting answers off the tops of our heads, but the reality is that knowing *where* (and often *how*) to find the answer is our real forte. Mary Goulding wrote about "the most exciting premise of reference services—that no one, not even the most experienced, knows all the answers; we are simply trained to use the vast network that helps us find them."[1] This "vast network" consists of colleagues, collections, catalogs, contacts, and more.

Once upon a time all a reference librarian had to do in order to provide good reference service was to memorize the titles and main features of the major reference books in each subject area. When asked a question, a quick run through that mental card file provided one or more titles that were sure to hold the answer—and usually did. The book—and it was always a book—was pulled from the shelf, pages were flipped through, and—voila! the answer was read or shown to the questioner. Today we—and our patrons—have many more choices (and formats) at our disposal. While anyone can "google" a query and find some kind of answer, what the reference librarian adds to the search is the ability to determine the most appropriate and authoritative source to use in order to find an accurate answer.

Just as architects use drawings and accountants use spreadsheets, reference librarians use reference sources; they are among the tools of our trade. And just as architects and accountants often use computers to create drawings and spreadsheets, reference librarians often use online sources.

What is a reference source? Although you might say that nearly anything could be a reference source—the daily newspaper, a website, a train schedule, or a recipe on the back of a box or can—here is how the *ALA Glossary of Library and Information Science* defines one: "Any source used to obtain authoritative information in a reference transaction. Reference sources can include printed materials, but are not limited to databases, media, the Internet, other libraries and institutions, and persons both inside and outside the library."[2]

Reference books are probably the most familiar type of reference source found in every library. What, exactly, is a reference book? Again, the *ALA Glossary* provides a definition: "1. A print or electronic book designed by the arrangement and treatment of its subject matter to be consulted for definite items of information rather than to be read consecutively."[3] For the discussion in this section, this definition is the one to keep in mind.

Although the world of reference publishing may be shrinking in terms of the number of reference publishers (because of corporate mergers and acquisitions), in terms of the number of reference titles published, it continues to expand. How can you keep current? Reading reviews is one way, and in our field we are fortunate that most reviews of reference sources are written by reference librarians who examine titles not only with the critical eye of a reviewer but also through the experienced eyes of a practitioner. Reference sources are regularly reviewed in the following publications: *Reference Books Bulletin*, a section of

✓ Some Reference Tips

- Familiarize yourself with reference sources by taking a look at the *Enoch Pratt Free Library Brief Guide to Reference Sources, Reference Sources for Small and Medium-Sized Libraries,* and *Guide to Reference.*
- Visit the reference section of your local public library or a college or university library and see how many of the titles mentioned in this chapter you can find.

ALA's *Booklist*, in which reviews are written by members of the *Bulletin's* editorial board as well as by contributing reviewers; *Library Journal*, in which reviews are written by current and former librarians; ALA's *Choice*, in which reviews are written by and for academic librarians; and *Reference and User Services Quarterly* (RUSQ), a publication of ALA's Reference and User Services Association (RUSA), in which reviews are written by volunteer librarians. Regular perusal of these publications, in which reviewers are encouraged to compare new titles with existing works, will keep you well informed.

> **Interested in how reference works are created?**
> *Distinguished Classics of Reference Publishing*, edited by James Rettig (Oryx, 1992), traces the history of some of the most notable reference books ever published.

There are also a number of reliable publications that recommend and review reference titles on a larger scale: The purpose of the *American Reference Books Annual* (ARBA) "is to provide comprehensive coverage of English-language reference books published in the United States and Canada during a single year."[4] Since 1970, ARBA has provided thousands of reviews written by hundreds of subject specialists and library professionals. In 2002 Libraries Unlimited, ARBA's publisher, launched *ARBAonline*, a database offering all the reviews published in ARBA's print version since 1997. The *Enoch Pratt Free Library Brief Guide to Reference Sources*, now in its tenth edition, is a compact, user-friendly handbook that "lists and discusses a selection of basic and popular reference works that are likely to be encountered in larger libraries in the United States today."[5] *Reference Sources*

> **Want to keep up with reference sources and trends?** Follow these blogs:
>
> *No Shelf Required*, www.libraries.wright .edu/noshelfrequired/
>
> *Points of Reference*, http://pointsof reference.booklistonline.com

for Small and Medium-Sized Libraries, now in its seventh edition, offers brief reviews of standard as well as recent reference works in a variety of formats written by members of the *Reference Sources for Small and Medium-Sized Libraries* Editorial Committee of the Collection Development and Evaluation Section of RUSA. One of the acknowledged classics of reference publishing, ALA's *Guide to Reference Books*, became the *Guide to Reference* in its twelfth edition and is now published in an electronic format only. Its contributing editors include subject experts representing a wide variety of academic and public libraries. Their concise annotations describe more than 16,000 print and electronic reference resources.

In part 1 I am going to review some of the most frequently used types of reference sources and discuss some specific titles. Among the types of reference sources to be considered are encyclopedias, dictionaries, websites, and directories. A list of all reference sources mentioned will be found after the bibliography.

Notes

1. Mary Goulding, "Real Librarians Don't Play Jeopardy," *Illinois Libraries* 77, no. 2 (1991): 142.
2. Michael Levine-Clark and Toni M. Carter, eds., ALA *Glossary of Library and Information Science*, 4th ed. (Chicago: American Library Association, 2012), s.v. "reference source."
3. Ibid., s.v. "reference book."
4. *American Reference Books Annual*, vol. 37 (Santa Barbara, CA: Libraries Unlimited, 2006), xiii.
5. Thomas H. Patterson, John A. Damand, and Rachel Kubie, *Enoch Pratt Free Library Brief Guide to Reference Sources*, 10th ed. (Baltimore, MD: The Library, 2000), xii.

Encyclopedias

It's the E-N-C-Y-C-L-O-P-E-D-I-A. Just look inside this book
and you will see, everything from "A" clear down to "Z."

—Jiminy Cricket

KENNETH KISTER DEFINES an encyclopedia in less Disneyesque terms: "An encyclopedia is a reference source published in either print or electronic form that summarizes basic knowledge and information on all important subjects or, in the case of a specialized encyclopedia, a particular subject."[1] An encyclopedia is often the best place to start when you are attempting to answer a question about a topic that is new or unfamiliar to you. Even when you are familiar with a subject—or actually know a specific fact—an encyclopedia can provide a quick, accurate, and authoritative answer. Just as there are reference librarians who are subject specialists and reference librarians who are generalists, there are encyclopedias which focus on a single subject and those which cover all subjects.

General Encyclopedias

General encyclopedias are probably the most familiar type of encyclopedia. Although today there are fewer general encyclopedias in print than there were a decade ago, publishers are still producing them, often along with an online version. Among general encyclopedias, the large, multivolume sets are the most prominent, although there are also some single-volume general encyclopedias.

In my experience, which has consisted mainly of providing general reference service, I am most familiar with what I like to think of as the "Big Three" of encyclopedias: the *Encyclopaedia Britannica*, *Encyclopedia Americana*, and the *World Book Encyclopedia*. I've listed them in order of size, from largest to the smallest, but a more accurate listing might be one done in terms of frequency of use. In that case, reverse the order: in a general reference setting, particularly in a telephone ready-reference service, the *World Book Encyclopedia* is one of the most frequently consulted reference works. Even now with the plethora of online sources available (among them *World Book Online*), there is nothing like opening a volume of the *World Book* and knowing you will find that list of the seven wonders of the world or a basic explanation of how a bill becomes a law. When I'm looking for a little more on a subject, perhaps an overview as well as a short bibliography, the *Encyclopedia Americana* would be my choice. And when I'm in search of even more, perhaps a detailed outline or history of a particular concept or place, as well as a substantial bibliography, the *Encyclopaedia Britannica* would be the one I consult. At this point I should also mention that both the *World Book Encyclopedia* and *Encyclopaedia Britannica* are available in online versions (*World Book Online* and *Britannica Online*) as well as print versions. Britannica recently announced that the 2010 print edition will be its last version in print. The last print edition of *Encyclopedia Americana* was published in 2006; there is an online version of *Americana* within *Grolier Online*.

These are my personal favorites; there are other encyclopedias available, among them *Compton's by Britannica* and *The New Book of Knowledge*. One of the best ways to keep current with the world of encyclopedia publishing is to read *Reference Books Bulletin*'s "Encyclopedia Update" published annually in the September 15 issue of *Booklist*. The authors look at both print and online encyclopedias and begin each update with a brief look at the state of encyclopedia publishing. These updates include careful evaluations of the scope, content, and functionality of the latest print and online encyclopedias. *Purchasing an Encyclopedia: 12 Points to Consider* (Booklist Publications/ALA, 1996) reprints the 1995 "Encyclopedia Update." Those twelve points are authority, arrangement, subject coverage, accuracy and objectivity, recency, approach, style, bibliographies, illustrations, multimedia, physical format, and yearbooks and other special products. These considerations are useful not only in purchasing an encyclopedia, but in selecting an encyclopedia to use in a particular reference situation.

Kenneth Kister offers the following points for consideration when evaluating an encyclopedia:

1. Does the encyclopedia provide the material you and others who will be using it are likely to need?
2. Is the encyclopedia comprehensible to you and others who will be using it?
3. Is the encyclopedia produced by reputable people?
4. Is the encyclopedia reliable?
5. Is the encyclopedia free from bias and stereotype?
6. Is the encyclopedia reasonably current?
7. Is the encyclopedia easy to use and are its contents readily accessible?
8. Does the encyclopedia include well-selected bibliographies?
9. Is the encyclopedia adequately illustrated?
10. Is the encyclopedia in book version physically well made and aesthetically pleasing?
11. Does the encyclopedia offer any special or unique features?
12. Is the encyclopedia available in both print and electronic form, and, if so, which do you want?
13. Is the encyclopedia fairly priced?
14. What do published reviews say about the encyclopedia?
15. How does the encyclopedia compare with its major competitors?[2]

Again, although some of these points may be of more concern to individuals purchasing an encyclopedia, either for a library collection or home use, many more of them should be of interest to someone deciding on a reference source to consult.

Specialized Encyclopedias

There are specialized encyclopedias covering almost any topic imaginable: just try a keyword search using "encyclopedia" and the subject of your choice in *BooksInPrint.com* or any online library catalog and look at the results. Specialized encyclopedias may be scholarly or popular in nature and single- or multivolume in format. Here are some examples of specialized encyclopedias chosen to illustrate the variety of subjects covered:

All Things Austen: An Encyclopedia of Austen's World. A tour of the beloved writer's milieu.

American Medical Association Concise Medical Encyclopedia. A consumer medical reference book offering 3,000 entries on illnesses, nutrition, parts of the body, and numerous other topics.

The Baseball Encyclopedia: The Complete and Definitive Record of Major League Baseball. 10th revised edition. A classic sports reference book that documents "America's pastime."

Benet's Reader's Encyclopedia. 5th edition. A one-volume companion to world literature first published in 1948.

Encyclopaedia Judaica. 2nd edition. 22 vols. An award-winning, landmark work of scholarship devoted to all aspects of Jewish history, culture, and religion. Available online as part of the Gale Virtual Reference Center.

Encyclopedia of Chicago. A comprehensive one-volume work with many special features produced under the auspices of the Chicago History Museum, the Newberry Library, and Northwestern University. Also available online at www.encyclopedia.chicagohistory.org.

Encyclopedia of Hair: A Cultural History. Examines hair as an indication of social class, gender, ethnicity, and more.

Encyclopedia of Popular Music. 4th edition. 10 vols. A multivolume look at popular music in all its forms from 1900 to the present.

Encyclopedia of Southern Culture. All aspects of southern life and lore are examined in this award-winning, single-volume work of scholarship.

Encyclopedia of Television. 2nd edition. 4 vols. Published under the auspices of the Museum of Broadcast Communications, this multivolume set offers hundreds of entries on many facets of the medium. The text of the 1st edition is available on the museum's website at www.museum.tv.

Encyclopedia of the Library of Congress: For Congress, the Nation and the World. Essays on the library's collections, articles on its buildings and history, biographies of the Librarians of Congress and more in a single-volume encyclopedia on the largest library in the world.

Worldmark Encyclopedia of the Nations. 12th edition. 5 vols. Since its first one-volume edition published in 1960, this has remained a standard reference work on the countries of the world. Available online as part of the Gale Virtual Reference Library.

A Word about *Wikipedia*

Wikipedia (www.wikipedia.org) is the online "free encyclopedia that anyone can edit." In the last ten years, *Wikipedia* has become one of the most frequently visited sites on the Internet. It has also generated considerable discussion among reference practitioners. In *Reference and Information Services: An Introduction*, Melissa A. Wong notes that, "although librarians should be wary of consulting *Wikipedia* for ready-reference factual information, the encyclopedia can be a valuable resource for general background information and pre-research information."[3] In an article entitled "Wikipedia: Friend or Foe?" Kathy West and Janet Williamson reported on a study undertaken "to assess whether Wikipedia can be used and recommended as a credible reference or information tool."[4] They concluded that "like any knowledge source, it should not be used in isolation from other sources of information. It is one tool in our information toolkit."[5] In other words, *Wikipedia* is *a* source, not *the* source. Casper Grathwohl considers the use of *Wikipedia* as a way to begin research on the Web. He writes that

Reference Tip

One way to evaluate an encyclopedia is to take a topic and look it up in several different encyclopedias and consider how it is treated in each. This can be particularly enlightening if you choose a controversial topic.

> through user-generated efforts, Wikipedia is comprehensive, current, and far and away the most trustworthy Web resource of its kind. It is not the bottom layer of authority, nor the top, but in fact the highest layer without formal vetting. In this unique role it therefore serves as an ideal bridge between the validated and unvalidated Web.[6]

Notes

The chapter epigraph is from Lorraine Santoli, *The Official Mickey Mouse Club Book* (New York: Hyperion, 1995), 135.

1. Kenneth Kister, *Kister's Best Encyclopedias: A Comparative Guide to General and Specialized Encyclopedias* (Phoenix: Oryx, 1994), 3.
2. Ibid., 17–20.
3. Melissa A. Wong, "Encyclopedias," in *Reference and Information Services: An Introduction*, 4th ed., ed. Richard E. Bopp and Linda C. Smith (Santa Barbara, CA: Libraries Unlimited, 2011), 544.
4. Kathy West and Janet Williamson, "Wikipedia: Friend or Foe?" *Reference Services Review* 37, no. 3 (2009): 260.
5. Ibid., 270.
6. Casper Grathwohl, "Wikipedia Comes of Age," *Chronicle Review*, January 7, 2011, http://chronicle.com/article/Wikipedia-Comes-of-Age/125899/.

TWO

Websites

Doing research on the Web is like using a library
assembled piecemeal by packrats and vandalized nightly.

—Roger Ebert

A LTHOUGH THE PICTURE is not quite this bleak here in the twenty-first century (Ebert's comment is from 1998), the old saying that the Internet
is "a mile wide and an inch deep" still rings true. Nevertheless the Web can
often be the best place to find the answer to a specific question or a source for
further information about a topic. However, reference librarians need to be
able to do more than just "google" a question. We need to know how to locate
accurate and authoritative websites both to answer patrons' specific questions
and to recommend to them for their own research. William A. Katz wrote that
"reference librarians are the Lewis and Clark of the vast Net territory."[1] And so
we are! Our profession includes a number of explorers and mapmakers who
have provided us with the charts and maps we need to navigate this wide,
wide world. Some of these are treated below.

MARS: Emerging Technologies in the Reference Section of ALA's Reference
and User Services Association has been recognizing outstanding reference websites for the last twelve years. The MARS Best Free Reference Websites Committee compiles an annual list of the best reference websites that is published
in *Reference and User Services Quarterly*. Among the selection criteria used are

1. Quality, depth, and usefulness of content
2. Ready reference
3. Uniqueness of content
4. Currency of content
5. Authority of producer
6. Ease of use
7. Customer service
8. Efficiency
9. Appropriate use of the Web as a medium[2]

A point-by-point explanation of these criteria as well as a combined index of the annual lists may be found at www.ala.org/rusa/sections/mars/marspubs/marsbestindex/. Reviews of web-based resources may also be found in the standard reference reviewing media, including *Choice*, *Reference Books Bulletin*, *Reference and User Services Quarterly*, and *Library Journal*.

The *Scout Report* (http://scout.wisc.edu/Reports/ScoutReport/Currrent/), the flagship publication of the Internet Scout Project based at the University of Wisconsin–Madison, is a weekly dispatch available by e-mail and on the Web since 1994. Each issue typically groups recommended sites under "research and education," "general interest," and "network tools." There is also a featured news article. The *Scout Report* is a convenient current awareness tool that offers website annotations prepared by a team of librarians and subject specialists. It uses the following criteria when evaluating websites:

- content
- authority
- information maintenance
- presentation
- availability
- cost

For further discussion of each criterion, go to http://scout.wisc.edu/Reports/selection.php.

In the early 1990s, Carole Leita, a reference librarian in Berkeley, California, began a bookmark file of useful and reliable free websites. The project grew as volunteer reference librarians from California added their selections, and the result was a dynamic, database-driven website of more than 20,000 entries known as the *Librarians' Internet Index* (LII). It would eventually receive funding from the Library Services and Technology Act. Its mission was "to provide a well-organized point of access for reliable, trustworthy, librarian-selected websites, serving California, the nation, and the world."[3] There were five main criteria used in the selection of entries, known as LII's "Big Five Factors":

1. Availability
2. Credibility
3. Authorship
4. External links
5. Legality[4]

In addition, potential LII entries were examined for

1. Authority
2. Scope and audience
3. Content
4. Design
5. Function
6. Shelf life[5]

If any of these criteria look familiar, and they should, remember that they were used by teams of librarians in the same way they might use Kenneth Kister's or *Reference Books Bulletin's* benchmarks (see chapter 2) in the selection of an encyclopedia. The *Librarians' Internet Index* lived up to its motto, "Websites you can trust."

In 2008, LII began to be hosted at The iSchool at Drexel College of Information Science and Technology as part of the process of its merging with the *Internet Public Library* (IPL).

The IPL originated in a graduate seminar at the University of Michigan's School of Information and Library Studies in 1995. In its mission statement it was defined as

> a global information community that provides in-service learning and volunteer opportunities for library and information science students and professionals, offers a collaborative research forum, and supports and enhances library services through the provision of authoritative collections, information assistance, and information instruction for the public.[6]

Now, as *ipl2: Information You Can Trust*, the IPL and the LII have been combined to form a website offering an array of resources and services (www.ipl2.org) that are definitely worth a look.

Most of this chapter has been devoted to discussing helpful and useful sources for locating reputable, free, and high-quality websites. As I've mentioned previously, many reference sources are available as web-based products. Most are fee-based, so in addition to the various criteria for selection already discussed, the issue of pricing needs to be considered. Unlike printed reference works, for which there is a one-time fee (price), web-based products usually involve licensing agreements of some kind in which the actual price paid may depend on the number of users in a library's service area, the number of full-time equivalent students at the institution, and so on. Since 1999, *The Charleston Advisor* (TCA; www.charlestonco.com) has provided critical reviews of web-based electronic resources. Both free and fee-based sources are included; for example, the April 2008 issue of TCA includes reviews of *Reference USA*, *Book Review Digest Plus* and *Book Review Digest Retrospective*, and *Value Line Research Center* (all fee-based), as well as of the *Consumer Action Web Site*, *World Cat*, and *The International Dunhuang Project: The Silk Road Online*, all freely accessible. The reviews are written by library and other information professionals and

---

Tips for keeping up with the wide world of the Internet:

- *Look* at your own library's website or those of other libraries. There are a variety of approaches to website design and function.
- *Subscribe* to the *Scout Report*. The weekly updates are a welcome addition to anyone's e-mail in-box.
- *Read* the professional literature, including *The Charleston Advisor, Reference Books Bulletin, Choice, RUSQ,* and *Library Journal,* for reviews of new websites and web-based sources as well as reconsiderations of familiar ones.
- *Explore* some of our national cyber treasures, such as the websites of the Library of Congress (www.loc.gov) and the Smithsonian Institution (www.smithsonian.org).
- *Browse* newspapers on the Web: local, national, and international. As print sales decline, most news organizations are putting more emphasis on their web content.

use a rating system which will score each product based on four elements: content, searchability, price, and contract options/features. A Comparative Score averaging these elements will provide an "at a glance" rating which will be prominently displayed near the top of each review.[7]

TCA reviews are critical as well as descriptive and include screen shots of the products under consideration.

The *Internet Library for Librarians* (www.itcompany.com/inforetriever/) is a commercial site established in 1994. As an information portal, it provides links to more than 3,000 web resources of interest to librarians: "All the resources are recommended, selected, and reviewed by librarians. Each entry has a full description of the goals and/or scope of the resource, as well as the contact information if provided."[8] There are ready-reference sites, sites devoted to specific areas of librarianship, such as acquisitions, cataloging and reference, library associations, journals, job opportunities, and much more.

This chapter has considered sources which reference librarians can use to locate useful and credible websites and web-based sources. In the succeeding chapters, specific online resources will be included in the discussions of particular types of reference sources (e.g., dictionaries, directories, etc.).

Notes

The chapter epigraph is from Roger Ebert, "Critical Eye," *Yahoo! Internet Life,* September 1998, 66.

1. William A. Katz, *Introduction to Reference Work*, 8th ed., vol. 1, *Basic Information Services* (New York: McGraw-Hill, 2002), 40.
2. "Best Free Reference Web Sites Combined Index, 1999–2011," RUSA Machine-Assisted Reference Section (MARS), www.ala.org/rusa/sections/mars/marspubs/marsbestindex/.
3. *ipl2,* www.ipl.org/div/about/LII_About/selectioncriteria.html.
4. Ibid.
5. Ibid.
6. *ipl2,* www.ipl.org/div/about/mission_and_vision.html.
7. *The Charleston Advisor* 9, no. 4 (2008): 4.
8. *Internet Library for Librarians,* www.itcompany2.com/inforetriever/about.htm.

THREE

Dictionaries

I've been in *Who's Who*, and I know what's what, but it'll be the first time I ever made the dictionary.

—Mae West

DICTIONARIES MAY WELL be the only basic reference tools used more frequently than encyclopedias. A dictionary, especially one of the unabridged kind, is simply one of the most useful reference sources to have on hand. Like encyclopedias and reference librarians, there are both general and specialized varieties of dictionaries. William A. Katz wrote about "eight generally accepted categories [of dictionaries]":

1. General English language dictionaries, which include unabridged titles (i.e., those with over 265,000 entries) and desk or collegiate dictionaries (from 139,000 to 180,000 entries). These are for adults and children.
2. Paperback dictionaries which may have no more than 30,000 to 55,000 entries and are often used because they are inexpensive and convenient to carry.
3. Historical dictionaries that show the history of a word from date of introduction to the present.

4. Period or scholarly specialized titles that focus on a given time period or place, such as a dictionary of Old English.

5. Etymological dictionaries that are like historical dictionaries, but tend to put more emphasis on analysis of components and cognates in other languages.

6. Foreign language titles, which are bilingual in that they give the meanings of the words in one language in another language.

7. Subject works which concentrate on the definition of words in a given area, such as science and technology.

8. "Other" dictionaries, which include everything from abbreviations to slang and proper usage.[1]

In this chapter, I'd like to focus on a few of Katz's categories, specifically, general English language dictionaries, historical dictionaries, subject works, and "other" dictionaries, and take a brief look at some examples of each.

General Dictionaries

When most people think of dictionaries, what comes to mind are either massive, unabridged dictionaries or their less cumbersome counterparts, desk dictionaries. These general dictionaries provide a plethora of information: pronunciations, definitions, synonyms and antonyms, derivations, and so on. The additional features often found in general dictionaries, especially the large ones, such as lists of signs and symbols, guides to proofreaders' marks, charts of language families, tables of weights and measures, and even maps of constellations, are also useful.

Webster's Third New International Dictionary, Unabridged sets the standard for a one-volume, unabridged dictionary. Comprehensive, authoritative, and reliable, it supplies etymologies and representative quotations. It does not include geographical or biographical names among its entries. The online version (http://unabridged.merriamwebster.com) contains a number of special features (audio pronunciation, a daily crossword puzzle, and word of the day) as well as material from other dictionaries produced by Merriam-Webster. *Random House Webster's Unabridged Dictionary* (2nd edition) is another reliable unabridged dictionary that includes geographical and biographical names and emphasizes contemporary usage. The *American Heritage Dictionary of the English Language* (4th edition) is one of the handiest reference tools around;

this desk dictionary offers more than 200,000 entries, and among its special features are full-color illustrations and an abundance of illustrative quotations. The *Oxford English Dictionary* (2nd edition, 20 vols.), or OED, is the greatest wordbook of our language and its foremost historical dictionary. Here you will find thousands of words explained in exhaustive entries tracing their use and meaning from Chaucer's day to our own. The *Oxford English Dictionary Online* (www.oed.com) includes all the material in the print edition as well as yearly additions and numerous new entries, as well as revisions of old ones.

Subject Dictionaries

Dictionaries that concentrate on the vocabulary of particular subjects or fields of study are widely available. The following are some examples.

Although there are many crossword puzzle aficionados who would shudder at the thought of consulting a dictionary (or using a pencil), there are probably just as many who don't mind getting a little help now and then. Crossword puzzle dictionaries may well be their reference work of choice. The *Random House Webster's Crossword Puzzle Dictionary* (4th edition) provides thousands of clues as well as answer words. *One Across.com* (www.oneacross .com) is an online tool that allows the puzzler to plug in the known letters, indicate spaces, and receive a list of possible word choices.

The "poet who doesn't know it" might be in need of a rhyming dictionary. One popular title is *Words to Rhyme With: A Rhyming Dictionary; Including a Primer of Prosody, a List of More Than 80,000 Words That Rhyme, a Glossary Defining 9,000 of the More Eccentric Rhyming Words, and a Variety of Exemplary Verses, One of Which Does Not Rhyme at All*. Entries in this comprehensive source are filed by rhyming sound rather than spelling. Would-be poets in cyberspace can turn to *RhymeZone* (www.rhymezone.com), which provides rhyming words, synonyms, definitions, and more.

Too many cooks might spoil the broth, but there aren't too many who won't find *The New Food Lover's Companion* (4th edition) to be a useful kitchen aid. More than 6,000 alphabetically arranged entries cover cooking tools, terms, and techniques. An appendix provides seventy pages of helpful kitchen information (equivalents, substitutions, conversion formulas, etc.). A bibliography of cookbooks tops off this delightful dictionary. Cybercooks will find more than 4,000 terms from an earlier edition of this work at *Food Dictionary* (www.epicurious.com/tools/fooddictionary/).

Other Dictionaries

Finally, here are some examples of Katz's "other" category of dictionaries. A visual dictionary, as defined by Joan M. Reitz, is

> a dictionary in which words and phrases (grouped by subject, theme, or activity) are illustrated, usually in a line drawing on the same or opposite page, with each term keyed to the corresponding feature in the diagram by a thin line or small reference number printed on the illustration.[2]

Two recent and well-received visual dictionaries are *Merriam-Webster's Visual Dictionary* and the *Ultimate Visual Dictionary*. Unlike a typical visual dictionary, Merriam-Webster's includes dictionary definitions. The *Ultimate Visual Dictionary* uses some 6,000 color photographs and illustrations.

Dictionaries of slang go where standard dictionaries may fear to tread: they include vulgar or socially unacceptable terms and colloquial words and define them in detail. *The New Partridge Dictionary of Slang and Unconventional English* (9th edition, 2 vols.) defines thousands of terms. It is a descendant of Eric Partridge's 1937 work, *The Dictionary of Slang and Unconventional English*.

Some of the most frequently asked reference questions involve acronyms and abbreviations. The *Acronyms, Initialisms and Abbreviations Dictionary* (44th edition, 4 vols.) is a standard reference tool that defines a wide variety of abbreviated forms found in a variety of fields. A companion title is the *Reverse Acronyms, Initialisms and Abbreviations Dictionary* (44th edition, 2 vols.), in which the actual term or organization is listed first, then the abbreviation or acronym. *Acronym Finder* (www.acronymfinder.com) is a free web tool that is also useful for this type of query.

Although the origins of words and phrases may certainly be found in unabridged or historical dictionaries, a more focused source is often easier to use. The *Facts on File Encyclopedia of Word and Phrase Origins* is actually an etymological dictionary offering thousands of entries.

Dictionaries

For more information about dictionaries, consult *Kister's Best Dictionaries for Adults and Young People: A Comparative Guide* (Oryx, 1992). Although the reviews of individual titles are now dated, the discussions about types of dictionaries, how they are compiled, and the field of lexicography are useful and informative.

Quotations are another frequently asked-about topic, and, I must admit, my favorite type of reference question. The definitive printed reference source for quotations is *Bartlett's Familiar Quotations* (17th edition). As each new edition of this classic work (first compiled in 1855 by John Bartlett) is published, material from previous editions often has to be omitted, so this is one case where all editions should be kept in the collection. There are many printed collections of quotations available, from all-purpose compilations to those of quotations about a specific subject. Oxford University Press has published a number of noteworthy titles, including the *Oxford Dictionary of American Quotations* (2nd edition), the *Oxford Dictionary of Modern Quotations* (2nd edition), and the *Oxford Dictionary of Quotations* (7th edition). Online compilations of quotations are also rampant; for recommendations of reliable websites, consult *ipl2* (www.ipl2.org).

Foreign-Language Dictionaries

Several publishers produce bilingual dictionaries that include English and another language. Among them are Larousse (www.houghtonmifflinbooks .com/larousse/), Harper Collins (www .harpercollins.com), and Oxford University Press (www.oup.com). Online sources include *Babel Fish* (babelfish .yahoo.com), where you can translate a web page or a block of text of up to 150 words, and *OneLook Dictionaries* (www.onelook.com), which offers a wide variety of online dictionaries that includes a number of foreign-language titles.

Notes

The chapter epigraph is from Elizabeth Knowles, ed., *Oxford Dictionary of Modern Quotations*, 2nd ed. (New York: Oxford University Press, 2002), 334.

1. William A. Katz, *Introduction to Reference Work*, 8th ed., vol. 1, *Basic Information Sources* (New York: McGraw-Hill, 2002), 378.
2. Joan M. Reitz, *Dictionary for Library and Information Science* (Westport, CT: Libraries Unlimited, 2004), 761.

FOUR

Almanacs, Handbooks, and Yearbooks

A calendar, a calendar! Look in the
almanack; find out moonshine.

—Shakespeare, *A Midsummer Night's Dream*, act 3, scene 1, line 55

T HE *ALA Glossary of Library and Information Science* uses the word *compendium* in defining almanacs, handbooks, and yearbooks:

Almanac—A compendium, usually an annual, of statistics and facts,
both current and retrospective. May be broad in geographical and
subject coverage, or limited to a particular country or state or to a
special subject.[1]

Handbook—A compendium, covering one or more subjects and of
basic or advanced level, arranged for the quick location of facts
and capable of being conveniently carried.[2]

Yearbook—An annual compendium of facts and statistics of the
preceding year, frequently limited to a special subject.[3]

What is a compendium? Joan M. Reitz defines a compendium as "a work
that treats a broad subject or entire field of knowledge briefly and concisely,
sometimes in the form of an outline."[4] The key, then, is that all these types of

books are brief and concise and concentrate on facts and statistics rather than narrative—just the thing when the question requires "just the facts, ma'am."

In order to illustrate the variety of almanacs, handbooks, and yearbooks available, I've chosen some representative titles for each category.

Almanacs

Almanacs are a mainstay of the general reference collection. Add a good general encyclopedia and an unabridged dictionary and you're ready to field almost any question.

The World Almanac and Book of Facts. Packed with facts and statistics of all kinds, this is an absolutely essential part of any reference collection. A detailed subject index and a concise quick reference index unlock the treasures within. It is available as an online database at OCLC's *FirstSearch*.

The Time Almanac. Known in previous editions as the *Information Please Almanac*, this is another reliable source of statistics and facts. A detailed subject index points the way to looked-for information.

Canadian Almanac and Directory. Published since 1847 by several different publishers, this is a key source of information on anything Canadian. Each of the seventeen sections includes a detailed table of contents. An online version is also available.

Whitaker's Almanack. First published in 1868, this classic reference work provides facts, figures, and functional information about the United Kingdom in particular and Europe and the rest of the world in general.

Our Sunday Visitor's Catholic Almanac. An annual volume that supplies doctrine, directory information, statistics, a liturgical calendar, and more.

Sports Illustrated Sports Almanac. This is the place to go for batting averages, yards run, championships won (and lost), and all the other myriad facts and factoids that sports fans crave.

The Old Farmer's Almanac. Between the familiar yellow covers of the oldest

> You can find *The Old Farmer's Almanac* online at www.almanac.com.

almanac published in the United States you'll find the phases of the moon, regional weather forecasts, recipes, gardening advice, and much more. U.S. and Canadian editions are available.

Handbooks

Handbooks are another essential component of any reference collection. They can provide an introduction to a subject, demystify terminology, or supply a chronology of facts or an array of statistics.

Famous First Facts: A Record of First Happenings, Discoveries, and Inventions in American History (6th edition). A classic reference work, Joseph Nathan Kane's unique creation offers more than 7,000 factual entries arranged under sixteen broad categories, with additional points of access through several indexes that make up half of the text. An electronic version is also available.

Notable Last Facts: A Compendium of Endings, Conclusions, Terminations and Final Events through History. A counterpart to *Famous First Facts* that supplies some 16,000 noteworthy ultimate facts organized by subject and augmented by an extensive table of contents and comprehensive index.

A Handbook to Literature (10th edition). A standard source of literary terminology and themes that also includes summaries of British and American literary history and appendixes listing Nobel (literature) and Pulitzer Prize (fiction, drama and poetry) winners.

Handbook of Denominations in the United States (13th edition). Covers the major religious traditions of Judaism, Christianity, and Islam practiced in the United States with brief histories, summaries of doctrine, and statistics.

CRC Handbook of Chemistry and Physics: A Ready-Reference Book of Chemical and Physical Data. A standard reference work that provides an array of physical and chemical data. Among the new tables in

> *Baseball Almanac* (www .baseball-almanac.com), "where what happened yesterday is being preserved today," is a privately held website with thousands of pages of baseball history, fast facts, and original research.

this edition are those covering the energy content of fuels and the atomic radii of elements. It is also available online and as an interactive DVD. See www.crcpress.com/product/isbn/9781439855119/ for more information.

Emily Post's Etiquette (18th edition). The classic handbook on good behavior has been updated to include modern concerns such as netiquette and cell phone courtesy. It is available online at www .emilypost.com.

Yearbooks

Yearbooks (no, *not* the ones with embarrassing pictures from your high school days) are another source of facts, events, and memorable moments from the year just passed.

Guinness World Records. What might be called the original "extreme" reference book: an annual guide to all that is largest, smallest, fastest, tallest, and much, much more. It includes a comprehensive subject index. On the Web visit www.guinnessworldrecords.com.

Chase's Calendar of Events. For more than fifty years, this has been the date book of choice for reference librarians and anyone else interested in commemorative days, weeks, months and years, holidays, anniversaries, astronomical phenomena, and more.

Broadcasting and Cable Yearbook. A comprehensive listing of thousands of AM and FM radio stations, television stations, and broadcasting industry service providers.

The Statesman's Yearbook 2011: The Politics, Cultures and Economies of the World (147th edition). Among the features in this acknowledged reference classic are biographical profiles, political histories, statistics, and economic overviews. Each print volume includes a special registration code that allows access to the online version.

Theatre World (66th edition). For more than sixty years this has been the yearbook of American theater seasons on Broadway, Off Broadway, Off-Off Broadway, and on regional stages.

The Library and Book Trade Almanac 2010 (formerly *The Bowker Annual*) (55th edition). Originally published by the R. R. Bowker Company and now by Information Today, this compilation of industry reports, statistics, news coverage and more has served librarianship and the book trade well since 1962. A noteworthy feature is an explanation of how to acquire an ISBN.

Yearbook of American and Canadian Churches. A source for statistics, descriptions of denominations, contact information about numerous religious organizations, a listing of religious periodicals, and more. The print version includes an online component.

Notes

1. Michael Levine-Clark and Toni M. Carter, eds., *ALA Glossary of Library and Information Science*, 4th ed. (Chicago: American Library Association, 2012), s.v. "almanac."
2. Ibid., s.v. "handbook."
3. Ibid., s.v. "yearbook."
4. Joan M. Reitz, *Dictionary for Library and Information Science* (Westport, CT: Libraries Unlimited, 2004), 164.

FIVE

Indexes

As index to the story we late talked of.

—Shakespeare, *Richard III*, act 2, scene 2, line 149

A N INDEX, AS defined in the *ALA Glossary of Library and Information Science*, is "a systematic guide to the contents of a file, document, or group of documents, consisting of an ordered arrangement of terms or other symbols representing the contents and references, code numbers, page numbers, etc., for accessing the contents."[1] Some of the most familiar types of these "systematic guides" were once available only in print, for example, the indexes found at the ends of books, the index volumes of encyclopedia sets, and indexes to newspapers and periodicals. For the most part, these print indexes are still available. In the case of newspaper and periodical indexes, however, online indexes now are more often the reference tool of choice. One of the advantages of using online indexes is that they often include abstracts of articles, and some of them include the full texts of articles as well as abstracts.

What is an abstract? The *ALA Glossary of Library and Information Science* defines an abstract as "an abbreviated, accurate representation of a work . . . accompanied by a bibliographic reference to the original work."[2] In other words, an abstract tells you exactly what an article is about in addition to providing its title and the title of the publication in which it appears and the issue and page numbers on which it will be found. This is a very useful feature when you are faced with a long list of articles to go through, and want to select only the most relevant.

One caveat about online newspaper indexes: for many titles, full retrospective indexing (say, before the 1960s) is not yet available. However, with the advent of digitization, online access to historical collections of newspapers is becoming more widely available.

Just as there are criteria for evaluating websites and print reference tools, there are some factors to keep in mind when choosing or using an index. In *Reference and Information Services: An Introduction*, Linda C. Smith lists several points to consider when evaluating an index. They are format, scope, authority, accuracy, arrangement, and special features.[3] Format can include such elements as the size of print, either on the page or on the screen, and the use of abbreviations and symbols (and their explanation). Scope refers to the time period and the kinds of publications indexed. Authority demonstrates the publisher's reputation for a product of high quality. Accuracy is reflected in entries that are complete, consistent, and correct. Arrangement refers to how entries are presented and how many different ways (i.e., author, title, subject, keyword) their contents may be accessed. Special features may include links to the full texts of articles and lists of subject terms used and publications indexed.

This chapter will discuss three kinds of indexes: general periodical indexes, newspaper indexes, and specialized indexes, and list some examples of each type.

General Periodical Indexes

The *Readers' Guide to Periodical Literature*, published by H. W. Wilson since 1900, is one of the most familiar reference tools to be found in just about any type of library. Always an indispensable part of the reference collection, it is now available in an online version as well as its familiar green monthly paperback issues and quarterly cumulations and annual hardcover volumes. *Readers' Guide* provides an author and subject index to nearly 400 general-interest periodicals. Online there are the *Readers' Guide Retrospective 1890–1982*, covering some 375 popular magazines; *Readers' Guide Full Text, Selection Edition*, providing full-text articles and indexing and abstracting for a wide selection of general periodicals; *Readers' Guide Abstracts*, offering indexing and abstracting for periodicals back to 1983; *Readers' Guide Full Text*, supplying full-text articles and indexing and abstracting beginning with 2005 issues of general periodicals; and *Readers' Guide Full Text, Mega Edition*, which delivers indexing of more than 400 magazines back to 1983, and full texts of articles back to 1994 from more than 200 journals, along with other special features, such as page images. These online products are continuously updated, and their coverage is updated and expanded in an ongoing program. In 2011, H. W. Wilson was acquired by EBSCO. Go to www .ebscohost.com for more information. Pro-Quest (www.proquest.com) produces a number of online sources for periodical research that offer indexing, abstracting, and the full texts of articles: *ProQuest Research Library* is a database offering access to the full text of articles from a wide assortment of trade publications, magazines, scholarly journals, and newspapers covering a broad range of subjects. *Periodicals Index Online* indexes several thousand journals in the arts, humanities, and social sciences from 1665 to 1995. Citations can link to the full-text articles in *Periodicals Archive Online*, another ProQuest database, or in other digital archives.

> **Reference Tip**
>
> How can you find out if a periodical is indexed? Entries in *Ulrich's International Periodicals Directory* include where each title is indexed.

Newspaper Indexes

Although there are print newspaper indexes with long publication histories, such as the *New York Times Index* (1913 to the present), many more newspapers were indexed for local content only, for example, by obituary card files maintained by local libraries, or not at all. Fortunately, digitization is changing this, and access to many more newspapers is now available online. Individual newspaper websites often offer online archives, with the full contents of articles sometimes available only to subscribers or for a fee.

> **Reference Tip**
>
> If you're trying to locate an article in a newspaper that has not been indexed, try searching in the print or online index of another newspaper. You may be able to pinpoint a date, and with that, go to the microfilm or paper copies of that newspaper.

ProQuest Newsstand offers a collection of 500 newspapers, 350 of them with full texts of their articles. It includes major national and international newspapers, and the coverage for many of them reaches back into the 1980s and 1990s. Libraries can select individual titles or choose from several subsets of databases (i.e., by region or state or ethnic interest). The *ProQuest Historical Newspapers* collection offers digitized versions of a number of newspapers, many of them dating back to the mid- and late nineteenth century and a few going even further back.

Specialized Indexes

There are also various special indexes offering access to specific subject areas and particular types of publications. Here are some examples: *Book Review Digest*, published by H. W. Wilson since 1905, is issued monthly (except February and July) and in quarterly and annual cumulations. It offers citations to and excerpts from the reviews of thousands of books each year published in more than 100 periodicals. *Book Review Index*, published by Gale Cengage, is issued three times a year in an annual cumulation. It provides citations to reviews from more than 900 publications and is also available online. *Play Index*, published by H. W. Wilson since 1949, helps the reader locate individual plays as well as plays in collections. Entries include such details as the size of the cast and the number of acts and scenes. *Short Story Index*, published by H. W. Wilson since 1900, is an annual publication indexing short stories in collections and periodicals. Both the *Play Index* and *Short Story Index* are available in print and online versions. The *Essay and General Literature Index*, published by H. W. Wilson since 1900, is issued twice a year and cumulated annually. It indexes essays, mainly in the social sciences and humanities, found in anthologies and collections. Wilson also publishes a number of other specific subject indexes, including *Art Index*, *Education Index*, and *Library Literature and Information Science Index*. Go to www.ebscohost.com for more information.

Reference Tip

How do you know which databases offer the full text of articles? Consult *Fulltext Sources Online*, published twice a year by Information Today, Inc., and also available in an online version (www.infotoday.com).

Notes

1. Michael Levine-Clark and Toni M. Carter, eds., *ALA Glossary of Library and Information Science*, 4th ed. (Chicago: American Library Association, 2012), s.v. "index."

2. Ibid., s.v. "abstract."

3. Linda C. Smith, "Indexes and Abstracts," in *Reference and Information Services: An Introduction*, 4th ed., ed. Richard E. Bopp and Linda C. Smith (Santa Barbara, CA: Libraries Unlimited, 2011), 614.

SIX

Directories

The list of those that claim their office this day.

—Shakespeare, *Henry VIII*, act 4, scene 1, line 14

O NE OF THE most useful kinds of sources in any general reference collection, directories may be used to answer some of the most frequently asked reference questions:

Who is the president and CEO of Trans-Global Mega-Corporation and how can I contact him/her?

Where is the headquarters of the Society for the Preservation of Gargoyles?

What is the name and contact information for a support group for people with two left feet?

All kidding aside, library patrons often need to know how to contact a company executive (ever try to find this kind of information on a website?) or where to find a support group for people with a particular medical condition or an organization dedicated to a specific social or political cause.

The *ALA Glossary of Library and Information Science* defines a directory in these precise terms: "A list of persons or organizations, systematically arranged, usually in alphabetic or classed order, giving address, affiliations, etc., for individuals, and address, officers, functions, and similar data for organizations."[1] Once available only in print, directories are now often also available in online versions, sometimes exclusively. As with many other kinds of reference sources, directories are most often dedicated to a certain type of information or a special subject. In *Reference and Information Services: An Introduction*, Joseph E. Straw offers several criteria for consideration when evaluating a directory. These include the scope of the directory, the currency of the information it supplies, the accuracy of that information, and its arrangement.[2]

As is the case with many other kinds of reference sources, directories can range from the very general to the very specific: there are simple name and address listings, for example, telephone directories; there are directories that supply contact information, for example, directories of corporations or organizations; and there are directories of specific fields or industries, for example, publications, libraries, and so on. In order to demonstrate the range of directories available, I've chosen a few of the kinds of directories most commonly found in general reference collections, specifically directories of libraries, directories of publications, and directories that focus on a single subject or field. But first I'd like to discuss two titles that don't quite fit into these categories; in fact, you might say that they are beyond categorization, but they are important parts of a general reference collection. They are *Directories in Print* and the *Encyclopedia of Associations*. *Directories in Print* (32nd edition, 3 vols.) includes more than 16,000 directories in its descriptive listings (volume 1) and indexes and cross-indexes them thoroughly in volume 2. The third volume is a supplement, periodically adding still more new listings.

The *Encyclopedia of Associations* (3 vols.) is an essential resource in any reference collection. This is the source to consult for information on more than 22,000 national membership organizations of all kinds, including those of social, political, religious, business, ethnic, fraternal, and avocational interest. Here you will find contact information, membership statistics, dates and locations of meetings or conventions, and the titles of publications and directories. Further coverage is available in the *Encyclopedia of Associations: International Organizations* and the *Encyclopedia of Associations: Regional, State and Local Organizations*. These volumes, and many other Gale directories, are also available online in the *Gale Directory Library* (www.gale.com/DirectoryLibrary/).

Libraries are part of the "vast network" mentioned in chapter 1, and in order to contact them it helps to have some sources on hand that provide the names of key staff members and descriptions of collections in addition to basic directory-type information. *The American Library Directory: A Classified List of Libraries in the United States and Canada, with Personnel and Statistical Data* supplies that and more, including listings of library schools, systems, networks, and consortia. Academic, public, and special libraries are listed geographically, starting with state or province, then city, then institution. Gale's *Directory of Special Libraries and Information Centers* supplies useful contact information for specialized subject collections around the world. Volume 2 of this work is entitled *Geographic and Personnel Indexes*, and there is now also a *Subject Directory of Special Libraries and Information Centers* in 3 volumes. These

> **Postal Directories on the Web:**
> The United States Postal Service (USPS) offers www.usps.gov, where you can find zip codes and post offices as well as purchase stamps and track packages. Canada Post at www.canadapost.ca provides similar services in English and in French.

directories are also part of the online *Gale Directory Library*. On the Web, Libweb (http://lists.webjunction.org/libweb/) provides links to "over 7,900 pages from libraries in 146 countries."

Another frequently asked-for type of information concerns publications of various kinds. Library patrons may want to write letters to editors, request back copies of magazines or newspapers, or order subscriptions. People purchasing books may need to verify authors, titles, publishers, or ISBN numbers. The *Gale Directory of Publications and Broadcast Media* (146th edition), formerly known as the *Ayer Directory of Publications*, is a standard reference work that supplies listings of radio stations, magazines, newspapers, and other publications in the United States and Canada. Entries are arranged geographically and include contact information, circulation figures, and more. It has a number of special indexes, including those by subject and type of publication as well as a master index. It is available online in the *Gale Directory Library*.

Another standard reference source for information about publications is *Ulrich's International Periodicals Directory*. This is a comprehensive and classified listing of periodicals that not only provides subscription and contact information but also indicates where a title is indexed, abstracted, and available online. It is thoroughly indexed by ISSN, subject, and title. Another important feature is the list of titles that have ceased publication since the last edition of the directory. It is also available online at www.ulrichsweb.com.

Books in Print is the source to consult when the question involves verifying a book's author, title, publisher, and so on. Once available only in print form, it is now also available online. The print version consists of seven volumes: the first six volumes list books by author and title and the seventh lists publishers. The 2010–2011 print edition of *Books in Print*, published by Grey House Publishing, contains more than a million listings of currently available books. There is also a *Subject Guide to Books in Print*, which consists of six volumes that classify books under Library of Congress subject headings. *BooksInPrint .com* provides all the bibliographic information supplied in the print version and more, including out-of-print and forthcoming titles. Many of the entries are annotated, many include reviews, and many include tables of contents and cover images.

Just like dictionaries and encyclopedias, there are directories for nearly every subject or field you might think of. Government, education, and business are three areas for which directory information is frequently requested: library patrons might be looking for contact information for elected officials or their staff members, for the location of cultural or educational institutions, or for the officers of corporations. Here are some representative directories for each of these areas. *The Europa World of Learning* (61st edition) offers international coverage of colleges, universities, museums, research institutes, and learned societies. The nations of the world are presented alphabetically, and under each one its various cultural and educational institutions are listed. All entries provide an address and telephone number and may also provide faculty and staff names and an institutional e-mail address. There is an alphabetical index of the institutions included at the end of the book. It is also available online at www.world oflearning.com.

The *Washington Information Directory* is a helpful work that has been

Telephone directories: Although print directories may become increasingly scarce, a reference collection should include a complete set of local telephone directories at the very least and those of other cities when the budget allows. Online directories include www.anywho.com and www.infospace.com. *Reference USA* (www.referenceusa.com) is a powerful database where directory information may be found. *Toll-Free Phone Book USA: A Directory of Toll-Free Telephone Numbers for Businesses and Organizations Nationwide* is published annually by Omnigraphics, Inc., and of course, you can always call 800-555-1212 to locate toll-free numbers.

published for several decades. It supplies contact information for numerous government agencies and congressional committees, as well as private and nonprofit organizations located in each district. Entries are arranged by broad subject area, and there are indexes by name as well as keyword/subject. An online version is also available as part of the CQ Press Political Contact Suite. Go to the CQ Press website at www.cqpress.com for further information.

Hoover's Business Press publishes a number of useful directories both in print and online. *Hoover's Master List of U.S. Companies* is a comprehensive annual publication providing information on some 10,000 companies in America. Public and private companies are listed, as are their subsidiaries and a number of associations, nonprofit organizations, government agencies, and foundations. Entries supply contact and basic information, stock symbols, and names of key executives. There are indexes searchable by stock symbol, industry, and headquarters location. Other Hoover titles are *Hoover's Handbook of World Business*, *Hoover's Handbook of Private Companies*, *Hoover's Handbook of American Business*, and *Hoover's Handbook of Emerging Companies*. *Hoover's Online* (www.hoovers.com) provides information from all the print directories and many other features.

Books and More

Amazon.com, www.amazon.com. Although it seems as if you can buy almost anything at Amazon.com, it remains a helpful site for the quick identification of books and their availability.

Alibris, www.alibris.com. This is an excellent source for older and out-of-print titles, be they books, music, or movies. Many libraries rely on it for filling in gaps in the collection.

WorldCat (www.worldcat.org) is an OCLC product that unlocks the riches of library catalogs worldwide.

Notes

1. Michael Levine-Clark and Toni M. Carter, eds., *ALA Glossary of Library and Information Science*, 4th ed. (Chicago: American Library Association, 2012), s.v. "directory."
2. Joseph E. Straw, "Directories," in *Reference and Information Services: An Introduction*, 4th ed., ed. Richard E. Bopp and Linda C. Smith (Santa Barbara, CA: Libraries Unlimited, 2011), 413.

SEVEN

Geographical Sources

Peering in maps for ports and piers and roads.

—Shakespeare, *Merchant of Venice*, act 1, scene 1, line 19

W HEN FACED WITH a geographical question, a reference librarian may more often be found peering at a computer screen rather than at a map printed on paper. Nevertheless there are still a number of print sources that, combined with online tools, will enable you to field any number of geographical queries.

William A. Katz noted that "no matter what format, geographical titles used in . . . reference may be subdivided into three large categories: maps and atlases, gazetteers, and guidebooks."[1] Joan M. Reitz defines a map as "any two-dimensional representation of all or a portion of the earth's surface . . . normally done to scale on a flat medium but increasingly in digital form."[2] She defines an atlas as "a bound or boxed collection of maps, usually related in subject or theme, with an index of place names (gazetteer) usually printed at the end."[3]

Maps and atlases are probably the most familiar kinds of geographical reference tools. From oversized volumes shelved in special atlas cases to the latest in electronic formats flickering on a computer monitor, there are a number of standard reference sources to consult when the question is "Where is . . . ?" or "How far is it to . . . ?"

Oxford's *Atlas of the World* (15th edition) is a highly regarded work which offers many special features, including city maps and census statistics, and is updated annually.

The *Oxford Atlas of the United States* (17th edition) includes charts, graphs, and statistics along with its outstanding collection of maps.

The *National Atlas of the United States* (www.nationalatlas.gov) "provides a comprehensive, maplike view into the enormous wealth of geospatial and geostatistical data collected for the United States." The federal government published a national atlas from 1874 until 1970. In 1997 Congress authorized the creation of a new national atlas and assigned the task to the United States Geological Survey. On this site you can customize maps for printing or viewing, print preformatted maps of various kinds, order wall maps, and use interactive maps.

The Perry-Castañeda Library Map Collection at the University of Texas at Austin (www.lib.utexas.edu/maps/) consists of some 250,000 maps, 11,000 of which are available online. All kinds of world, region, and country maps as well as various other types of maps (e.g., gas prices, elections) are available and may be downloaded. There are also links to many other map websites.

The United States Geological Survey (www.usgs.gov), "your source for science you can use," provides resources for biology, geography, geology, geospatial information, and water study.

Map Collections (http://memory.loc.gov/ammem/gmdhtml/) supplies digitized images from the Geography and Map Division of the Library of Congress. These maps are arranged into seven categories: "cities and towns," "conservation and environment," "discovery and exploration," "general maps," "cultural landscapes," "military battles and campaigns" and "transportation and communication."

There is no shortage of maps in cyberspace. Some of the most popular mapping sites include *Google Earth* (http://earth.google.com), *MapQuest* (www.mapquest.com), and *Mappy Road Guide* (www.mappy.com).

A gazetteer is defined by Joan M. Reitz as

> a separately published dictionary of geographic names that gives the location of each entry. Also, an index of the names of the places and geographic features shown in an atlas, usually printed in a separate section following the maps, with locations indicated by page number or map number and grid coordinates.[4]

The Columbia Gazetteer of the World (2nd edition) is a revision of a work that set the standard for a geographical reference work when it was published in 1998. (Its predecessor, the *Columbia-Lippincott Gazetteer of the World*, last published in 1961, was the original standard-bearer.) More than 170,000 entries packed into three volumes provide information on both the physical (e.g., oceans, mountains, lakes) and political (e.g., countries, cities, capitals) world. An online version (www.columbiagazetteer.org) is available.

In *Reference and Information Services: An Introduction*, David A. Cobb notes that the *Rand McNally Commercial Atlas and Marketing Guide* (2 volumes) "has long been considered an unofficial gazetteer for the U.S."[5] Offering census and economic data, specialized maps and comprehensive state indexes, this is one of the most practical of geographical reference sources.

Online, the *U.S. Gazetteer* (www.census.gov/cgi-bin/gazetteer/) from the United States Census Bureau is a helpful resource.

> When the question involves booking a flight or a hotel room, travel sites such as *Expedia* (www.expedia.com), *Travelocity* (www.travelocity.com), and *Orbitz* (www.orbitz.com) are very helpful.

Guidebooks are indispensable items for travel to an unfamiliar place and may be just as helpful in a reference setting.

The *Forbes Travel Guides* (formerly *Mobil Travel Guides*) series is one of the most useful for reference work or traveling. Other useful travel guidebooks include those published by *Fodor's Travel Guides* (www.fodors.com) and *Rough Guides* (www.roughguides.com). When using guidebooks, it is essential to consult the latest edition available since much of the information they provide is subject to change.

Notes

1. William A. Katz, *Introduction to Reference Work*, 8th ed., vol. 1, *Basic Information Services* (New York: McGraw-Hill, 2002), 420.
2. Joan M. Reitz, *Dictionary for Library and Information Science* (Westport, CT: Libraries Unlimited, 2004), 438.
3. Ibid., 49
4. Ibid., 308.
5. David A. Cobb, "Geographical Sources," in *Reference and Information Services: An Introduction*, 4th ed., ed. Richard E. Bopp and Linda C. Smith (Santa Barbara, CA: Libraries Unlimited, 2011), 570.

EIGHT

Biographical Sources

History is the story of innumerable biographies.

—Thomas Carlyle

O NE THING I'VE learned in my years as a reference librarian is that people are interested in other people, that is, in their birth and death dates, background, ethnicity, marital status, accomplishments, and so on. Celebrities, both living and dead, historical figures, sports heroes, world leaders, notorious criminals, entertainers, and many others are all a frequent subject of "Who is . . . ?" or "How old is . . . ?" questions. Biographical information can certainly be found in general reference sources such as encyclopedias, but for more detailed information it is often better to turn to a specifically biographical reference source. As is the case with many kinds of reference works, biographical reference sources may be very general, covering a wide variety of people, or very specific, focusing on the notables of one country or in a particular field. Perhaps more than any other type of reference source, the biographical reference work has undergone a significant change in format in recent years. As Jack O'Gorman and Sue Polanka note in the chapter on biography in *Reference Sources for Small and Medium-Sized Libraries*,

> The development of extensive online biographical resources has been a big change . . . *Marquis Who's Who on the Web*, *Biography*

Reference Bank, and other sources have changed biographical information from a largely print collection into an electronic one.[1]

The use of electronic reference sources such as the ones mentioned above offers flexibility in searching, from providing multiple points of access to the ability to simultaneously search more than one volume or edition of a specific biographical reference work.

Here are some examples of the variety of electronic biographical reference sources currently available:

Biography and Genealogy Master Index, or BGMI. Gale Cengage Learning (www.gale.com). Originally a print resource and now available in both print and electronic formats, the BGMI is a comprehensive tool that supplies citations to biographical entries in some 2,000 reference works. The sources cited include biographical dictionaries (including *Who's Who* titles published by Marquis), subject encyclopedias, literary criticism, and other indexes. This is an excellent place to start a search for biographical citations which can then be used to locate specific articles and entries. BGMI is updated twice a year in both formats.

Marquis Who's Who on the Web. Marquis Who's Who (www.marquis whoswho.com). Print volumes of *Who's Who in America*, *Who's Who in the World*, and *Who Was Who in America* have long been an essential part of a reference collection. The contents of these titles, and many more Marquis Who's Who publications from 1985 to the present, are included in this massive database. It is easily searched and updated daily, offering a rich resource for current and concise biographical information.

Biography in Context, or BIC. Gale Cengage Learning (www.gale.com). BIC provides the full texts of biographical articles from over 170 titles published by Gale. In addition, there are full-text articles from newspapers and magazines and other content.

Biography Reference Bank. H. W. Wilson Company. Another outstanding biographical reference resource is the *Biography Reference Bank* (www.ebscohost.com/public/biography-reference-bank/). Long regarded as a reliable publisher of essential library reference tools (e.g., *Readers' Guide to Periodical Literature*, *Current Biography*,

Famous First Facts), Wilson (now through EBSCO) here provides profiles, photos, articles, essays, and much more about one-half million people.

American National Biography Online, or ANB. American Council of Learned Societies and Oxford University Press (www.anb.org). In 1999, Oxford University Press and the American Council of Learned Societies (ACLS) produced the ANB in print and electronic formats. Before that time, the *Dictionary of American Biography* (DAB) was the premier source of biographical information about distinguished (and deceased) Americans. The DAB was published by Charles Scribner's Sons and the ACLS, and consisted of twenty volumes published between 1928 and 1936, an index issued in 1937, and supplements published from 1944 to 1985. Approximately 19,000 notable Americans in the DAB are profiled in scholarly sketches ranging in length from a few paragraphs to a few pages. The ANB features biographies of more than 17,000 Americans of note; some 10,000 of them who were featured in the DAB are represented here in new biographies. Some 7,000 individuals are also represented whose biographies did not appear in the DAB. The ANB is updated quarterly and is easily searched.

Even a quick scan of the lists of sources included in each of these online biographical sources will give you an idea of the vast number of titles that once had to be searched individually. Online sources offer a kind of "one-stop shopping" for the librarian or library patron in search of biographical information.

> **Reference Tip**
>
> Sometimes you don't need to conduct an in-depth search for biographical information. Sometimes the library's computers are down. What to do? Consult the *Almanac of Famous People* (9th edition). Here you will find brief biographical information and often citations to other sources on more than 30,000 individuals.

> **Another Reference Tip: An Old Favorite**
>
> One of the most useful, although admittedly dated, biographical reference books is *The New Century Cyclopedia of Names* (3 vols.). Here you will find fictitious and even mythological figures as well as historical ones. Works of literature, events, and places are also included.

Note

1. Jack O'Gorman, ed., *Reference Sources for Small and Medium-Sized Libraries*, 7th ed. (Chicago: American Library Association, 2008), 284.

NINE

Statistical Sources

There are three kinds of lies: lies,
damned lies, and statistics.

—Attributed to Benjamin Disraeli by Mark Twain

H OW MUCH," "HOW many," and "what percentage" are frequently asked questions at the reference desk. Statistics of all kinds, from the numbers representing housing starts and crimes committed to the figures charting population trends and retail sales, are eagerly sought by library patrons. As is the case with biographical and geographical reference sources, a search that once involved looking through numerous print volumes can now be conducted more quickly (but not necessarily more easily) by the use of online reference sources. The origin of a statistic should always be kept in mind: numbers compiled by an industry trade group might just possibly differ from statistics gathered by the governmental agency which regulates that industry. Currency is usually of the utmost importance for most statistics seekers, unless, of course, they are engaged in historical research.

Some of the areas in which statistics are frequently asked for include population, business, and health. What follows are examples of statistical reference sources in each of these areas, as well as examples of general statistical reference sources, ratings and rankings, and some miscellaneous statistical sources.

General Statistical Sources

In the chapter on government documents and statistics sources in *Reference and Information Services: An Introduction*, Eric Forte and Mary Mallory note that "the *Statistical Abstract of the United States* is at once both an index to statistical material and a source of statistics itself."[1]

Statistical Abstract of the United States. www.census.gov/compendia/statab/. If the question is about some current aspect of American life, there is probably a government agency that has counted it in some fashion. Once only a print source, the "Stat Abstract" was also available online. Effective October 1, 2011, the U.S. Census Bureau terminated the collection of data for the Statistical Compendium program, of which the *Statistical Abstract* was a part. Starting in 2013 ProQuest will publish the *Statistical Abstract* in print (with Bernan Press) and digital formats.

FedStats. www.fedstats.gov. Produced by the Federal Interagency Council on Statistics, this is a comprehensive index to the web versions of federal government statistical data collected by over 100 government agencies. It can be searched by topic, agency, or program and also includes links to a wide variety of other governmental and statistical sites, including the statistical agencies of other nations from Afghanistan to Zambia.

UNdata. http://data.un.org. Created by the Statistics Division of the UN's Department of Economic and Social Affairs, this site offers access to a variety of statistical databases compiled by agencies of the United Nations. These are official statistics collected by member nations and cover a number of concerns, among them agriculture, education, health, population, refugees, and trade and tourism.

Population Statistics

U.S. Census Bureau. www.census.gov. Demographic data collected by the U.S. Census Bureau with numerous links to other national and international statistical sites and many other online tools are offered at this site. It also features a population clock tracking our national numbers.

American FactFinder. http://factfinder2.census.gov/faces/nav/jsf/pages/index.xhtml. This is the portion of the census website to go to for detailed demographic data. The U.S. Population Clock ticks here as well.

Historical Census Browser. http://fisher.lib.virginia.edu/collections/stats/histcensus/. On this site the Geospatial and Statistical Data Center of the University of Virginia provides access to information taken from historical volumes of the U.S. Census of Population and Housing from 1790 to 1960.

Business Statistics

Bureau of Labor Statistics. www.bls.gov. This unit of the U.S. Department of Labor gathers data on inflation, prices, employment and unemployment, pay and benefits, productivity, and more. In addition, its website provides news releases and the latest index figures, including the Consumer Price Index (CPI), the unemployment rate, and the Producer Price Index (PPI).

County Business Patterns. www.census.gov/prod/www/abs/cbptotal .html. Here you will find reports on an assortment of areas in our economy, including manufacturing, transportation, public utilities, mining, forestry, retail trade, and more. This data is available back to 1993, and there are discrete annual accounts of economic activities in each state, the District of Columbia, and Puerto Rico.

Reference Tip

When using a general reference source, for example, the *World Almanac and Book of Facts*, for statistical information, note the source of the table or graph provided, and use that as a lead for possible further information.

Business Statistics of the United States: Patterns of Economic Change (15th edition). This annual publication provides a wide range of data drawn from federal government sources. It includes key economic indicators, such as gross domestic product, personal income, and employment and unemployment figures.

Handbook of U.S. Labor Statistics: Employment, Earnings, Prices, Productivity and Other Labor Data (13th edition). Another annual volume that provides information formerly offered by *Labor Statistics*, a discontinued publication of the Bureau of Labor Statistics. Here you will find historical as well as recent information on earnings, employment, prices, productivity, and more.

Health Statistics

National Center for Health Statistics, or NCHS, Centers for Disease Control and Prevention. www.cdc.gov/nchs/. This searchable website offers health statistics of all kinds, from the U.S. fetal mortality rate to the number of U.S. outpatient surgeries and much more. It also provides information about various NCHS initiatives, including surveys and research.

National Center for Health Statistics: Injury Data and Resources. www .cdc.gov/nchs/injury.htm. This is another component of the website listed above that supplies "injury morbidity and mortality data and statistics available from the National Center for Health Statistics." Figures on occupational and accidental injuries as well as deaths from those injuries are included.

National Cancer Institute, National Institutes of Health. www.cancer .gov/statistics/. The National Institutes of Health maintains SEER (Surveillance, Epidemiology, and End Results), a searchable database offering "information on cancer incidence and survival in the United States."

World Health Report, United Nations World Health Organization. www .who.int/whr/. The UN World Health Organization's annual report includes health statistics for countries around the globe. Each year's report focuses on a particular subject with relevant statistics. The report is also available in print.

Ratings and Rankings

America's Top-Rated Cities: A Statistical Handbook. Four volumes, each devoted to a region of the United States (southern, western, central, eastern), provide a wealth of statistical data for the cities so rated. Entries range in length from ten to twenty pages and include a variety of facts and figures, including cost of living, population, and taxes. Comparative statistics are included. The handbook is also available as an e-book.

America's Top-Rated Smaller Cities: A Statistical Handbook. A companion to *America's Top-Rated Cities: A Statistical Handbook* that offers the same kind of data about highly rated cities with populations between 25,000 and 125,000. It is also available as an e-book.

Education State Rankings: Pre-K–12 Education in the 50 United States. Compares state education statistics in a variety of categories, including reading and math scores, special education, class size, graduation rates, per-pupil spending, and more.

Business Rankings Annual. Since 1989 this annual publication has provided a wealth of business statistics in ranked lists of various kinds arranged by subject. Its entries include the source of the data, a helpful feature for further research. Each volume is indexed, and a separate cumulative index covering all volumes back to 1989 is also published. It is also available online as part of the *Gale Directory Library*.

> ### Sports Statistics
>
> What is it about sports fans and statistics? In the days before the Internet librarians relied on newspaper box scores, media guides issued by professional sports teams, and publications like *Sporting News*'s annual guides and registers for the major sports. Today sports statistics are easily found online: there are sites for every major sport (e.g., www.baseball-reference.com) and league (e.g., www.mlb.com), as well as sites of various kinds maintained by dedicated fans.

Miscellaneous Statistics

American Religion Data Archives. www.thearda.com. The Association of Religious Data Archives maintains this searchable database that provides membership and attendance statistics, national profiles, surveys, and a number of "quick lists" which link to other related sites.

Box Office Mojo. www.boxofficemojo.com. Provides daily, weekly, weekend, monthly, quarterly, seasonal, yearly, and all-time box office results.

ChildStats.gov. www.childstats.gov. The Federal Interagency Forum on Child and Family Statistics, "a working group of Federal agencies that collect, analyze, and report data on issues related to children and families," maintains this searchable site.

Bureau of Justice Statistics. www.ojp.usdoj.gov/bjs/. The U.S. Department of Justice's site for statistics about crime and victims, law enforcement, courts and sentencing, corrections, and so on, as well as reports on related issues.

Election Statistics. http://clerk.house.gov/member_info/electionInfo/. The Office of the Clerk, U.S. House of Representatives, collects and publishes the official vote counts for federal elections. This searchable site provides those figures going back to the election of 1920.

Injury Facts, National Safety Council. Known as *Accident Facts* from 1921 to 1998, this annual publication by the Research and Statistics Department of the National Safety Council (www.nsc.org) provides data on occupational, motor vehicle, home, and other accidents, as well as on nonfatal injuries and deaths.

Note

1. Eric Forte and Mary Mallory, "Government Information and Statistics Sources," in *Reference and Information Services: An Introduction*, 4th ed., ed. Richard E. Bopp and Linda C. Smith (Santa Barbara, CA: Libraries Unlimited, 2011), 681.

PART 2

Reference Services

The reference librarian is the library's human face.

—David Tyckoson, "That Thing You Do"

W HETHER THAT "HUMAN face" is a voice on the telephone, the reply to an e-mail, chat, or text message, or an actual human visage, the implication is the same: reference librarians *are* the library to the person in need of information. Our role is to help our patrons find what they seek, and often, help them figure out exactly what that is. One of the finest compliments I've ever received as a reference librarian was to hear a patron say, "You're the first person I've spoken to today who understands what I'm talking about."

Reference service demands a lot from its practitioners: a wide general knowledge, a sense of curiosity and willingness to learn, the ability to listen, familiarity with the collections and services offered by your institution as well as those of others nearby, a genuine desire to help, and the capacity to treat all library patrons (*and* your coworkers) with courtesy, interest, and respect. An unlimited supply of patience and a healthy sense of humor are also essential.

Reference service embodies a basic principle of librarianship—direct assistance to readers: we answer their questions, help them locate needed information, and guide them through our sometimes (make that *often*) confusing library systems. In 1876 Samuel S. Green called it "personal relations between librarians and readers."[1] He described four functions of reference

In 1876, in one of the earliest articles in library literature to discuss what we now call reference service, Samuel S. Green lays out its four fundamental principles. More than a century later, in 1997, Tyckoson considers contemporary reference service and finds that Green's four founding principles are still relevant today. Green, "Personal Relations between Librarians and Readers," *Library Journal* 1, nos. 2–3 (November 30, 1876): 74–81. Tyckoson, "What We Do: Reaffirming the Founding Principles of Reference Services." *Reference Librarian* 59 (1997): 3–13.

service: showing readers how to use the library, answering their questions, helping them select books, and promoting the library in the community. The *ALA Glossary of Library and Information Science* considers reference service to be synonymous with information service, and defines the latter as "information or research assistance provided to library users by library staff."[2]

In the following chapters I will discuss reference techniques and processes, some of the different types of reference services, and reference policies, standards, and evaluation.

Two excellent LIS textbooks have been recently updated, and both provide numerous suggestions for further reading: Richard E. Bopp and Linda C. Smith, eds., *Reference and Information Services: An Introduction*, 4th edition (Santa Barbara, CA: Libraries Unlimited, 2011); and Kay Ann Cassell and Uma Hiremath, *Reference and Information Services in the 21st Century: An Introduction*, 2nd revised edition (New York: Neal-Schuman, 2011).

Notes

1. Samuel S. Green, "Personal Relations between Librarians and Readers," *Library Journal* 1, nos. 2–3 (November 30, 1876): 74.
2. Michael Levine-Clark and Toni M. Carter, eds., *ALA Glossary of Library and Information Science*, 4th ed. (Chicago: American Library Association, 2012), s.v. "reference services," "information services."

TEN

The Reference Interview

Conducting a reference interview is the most
important work a reference librarian does, because
this enables the librarian to match the patron's
question to a relevant and useful source.

—Stephanie Willen Brown, "The Reference Interview"

W HAT IS THE reference interview? It is the process by which a reference
librarian, through a series of questions, determines exactly what the
patron is looking for. Why would you need to "interview" a library patron?
Don't you simply listen to the question and then answer it? Seasoned reference librarians will tell you that library patrons will often "hide" their actual
questions; for example, they ask "where are the history books" when what
they really want to know is the date of the Battle of Bull Run. Many people,
particularly adults, are afraid or ashamed to admit that they don't know something, and so will ask a very general question (where are the history books?)
when what they need to know is a specific fact (the date of the Battle of Bull
Run). The reference interview, then, is a process of communication, and a
singular one at that: one person (the patron) is attempting to tell another (the
librarian) what they *don't* know.

The *ALA Glossary of Library and Information Science* defines the reference
interview as "the interpersonal communication between a reference staff

member and a library user to determine the precise information needs of the user. Synonymous with question negotiation."[1] Joan M. Reitz offers this definition: "The interpersonal communication that occurs between a reference librarian and a library user to determine the person's specific information need(s), which may turn out to be different than the reference question as initially posed."[2]

So we've established that sometimes library patrons are hesitant about asking for what they really need to know, and that a reference interview should be conducted in order to draw them out. How do you conduct a reference interview? Is it a matter of playing "Twenty Questions"? Not exactly. ALA's Reference and User Services Association described the qualities and skills needed to conduct a reference interview in "Guidelines for Behavioral Performance of Reference and Information Services Providers" (see the appendix). They are approachability, interest, listening/inquiring, searching, and follow-up. The first version of these guidelines (1996) was mainly concerned with in-person reference service, and the latest version has been expanded to include remote reference services, that is, reference services offered by e-mail or chat or telephone. The discussion in this chapter will focus on the guidelines for reference service in a general sense; subsequent chapters will address in-person, telephone, and online reference in a little more detail.

Elaine Z. Jennerich and Edward J. Jennerich, *The Reference Interview as a Creative Art*, 2nd edition (Libraries Unlimited, 1997) approaches the reference interview as a "performance" requiring a particular set of skills.

Catherine Sheldrick Ross, Kirsti Nilsen, and Marie L. Radford, *Conducting the Reference Interview: A How-to-Do-It Manual for Librarians* (Neal-Schuman, 2009) is an in-depth look at the reference interview replete with numerous annotated citations to the professional literature.

Approachability

A person with a question needs to feel welcome and know that there is someone who can help. A welcoming presence is essential, whether that is an actual presence consisting of an engaged and attentive person at a reference desk (clearly visible and with appropriate signage) or a friendly, professional voice on the phone or an easily found link to an electronic reference service. The main idea here is that a person, who may be confused or intimidated, is put at his or her ease and is assured in some way that there is someone ready and willing to help.

Interest

The librarian must demonstrate that he or she is interested in the question and committed to providing assistance. Attention is focused on the patron, either with eye contact and verbal and nonverbal behaviors at an in-person service point, by timely written acknowledgments and responses in an online environment, or by a friendly, articulate voice on the telephone.

Listening/Inquiring

Good communication skills are essential for good reference service. The librarian must be able to listen carefully to the patron's question and respond in an encouraging way, asking questions to help clarify the request and ensure that it is completely understood. This applies to any form of reference service, whether in-person, on the phone, or online. In addition, the librarian must maintain his or her objectivity about the nature of the question and its subject matter.

Searching

This is where the librarian finds out where the patron has already looked and engages in a conversation that will result in an effective search strategy. For example, spelling can be verified, the level or amount of information needed can be determined, and so on. Often the librarian can explain the search process as it goes forward. For example, when checking the online catalog or a database, the librarian can turn the computer screen toward the patron and show the actual search.

Follow-Up

This step involves determining whether the question has been answered to the patron's satisfaction. At this point appropriate referrals to other sources may be made if the original question was not, in the patron's opinion, answered completely. These "other sources" may be other reference tools, another department in the library, or other libraries or institutions that may provide additional information or assistance.

Catherine Sheldrick Ross writes that

> a good reference interview is a collaboration. User and librarian are equal partners in the search, with different areas of expertise. The user is the expert in the question itself and knows how the question arose, what necessary information is missing in her understanding of the topic, and how the information will be used. The staff member is the expert on the library system and the organization and retrieval of information. Both need to work together.[3]

Notes

1. Michael Levine-Clark and Toni M. Carter, eds., *ALA Glossary of Library and Information Science*, 4th ed. (Chicago: American Library Association, 2012), s.v. "reference interview."
2. Joan M. Reitz, *Dictionary for Library and Information Science* (Westport, CT: Libraries Unlimited, 2004), 601.
3. Catherine Sheldrick Ross, "The Reference Interview: Why It Needs to Be Used in Every (Well, Almost Every) Reference Transaction," *Reference and User Services Quarterly* 43, no. 1 (2003): 38.

ELEVEN

Reference Service in Person

When you're listening to a patron, nothing is more important. Not the patron you just finished helping or the patron next in line, but the one who needs you right now. Every patron deserves all your attention and interest.

—Donna M. Fisher, "The Important of Being Ear-Nest"

W HEN WORKING AT a reference desk, you may have to perform a balancing act between answering a phone and helping a person right in front of you. Even if you are fortunate, as I have been, to work mostly at reference desks where you don't have to also answer a phone and can direct all your attention to the people in front of you (the reference telephones are in a separate area), providing reference service in person requires a considerable degree of finesse. For the sake of this discussion, I'll use the model I'm most familiar with, a reference desk where all the attention can be focused on patrons in the library. The RUSA behavioral guidelines recommend that at the reference desk you should be "poised and ready to engage approaching patrons. The librarian is aware of the need to stop all other activities when patrons approach and focus attention on the patron's needs" (1.2). How can you appear "poised and ready to engage approaching patrons"? The answer can be summed up in just two words: body language. When working at the reference desk, sit up straight, constantly scan the room for patrons, make eye contact with them, maybe even stand up (!)—or walk over to them and ask if you can help. To put it bluntly, the patron is not an interruption of your work, the patron *is* your work. If there were no patrons to ask questions, there would be no need for a reference librarian!

Of course, there will be occasional slow periods at the reference desk, and those are times for another balancing act—you don't want to sit there staring into space, nor do you want to have your head buried in reading material or your eyes glued to a computer screen. Look up frequently—not only will you notice an approaching patron, but you'll give your eyes a rest. It's usually a good idea to bring something to the desk—a professional journal or news magazine or some easily interruptible paperwork. I've found that the likelihood of a busy shift at the reference desk is in direct proportion to the amount of work you bring out: the more work you bring out, the busier your shift will be. Downtime at the reference desk also offers an opportunity to explore your library's website, try out a new database or other online tool, read news feeds, online journals, and so on. This is not the place, however, to get engrossed in personal e-mail or online shopping! The more familiar you are with your library's online services as well as the Internet in general, the better you will be able to help patrons.

Busy times at the reference desk require yet another balancing act: you may be faced with a number of patrons, all clamoring for your attention. Simply asking "who's next?" will go a long way toward "crowd control," and in most situations, the people waiting know very well whose turn it is! When you're helping a patron and notice someone waiting behind them, catch their eye—it will signal that you know they are there and are waiting. In some cases, particularly with a long line, saying to the waiting patrons, "I'll be with you as soon as I can," and, as each person steps up to the desk, saying "Thank you for waiting," will also go a long way in demonstrating your interest in them and their questions.

Sally Decker Smith and Roberta Johnson, "Reference Desk Realities," *Public Libraries* 46, no. 1 (January 2007): 69–73. Smith and Johnson describe working at a public library reference desk with gentle humor and sage advice.

This discussion has focused on working solo at the reference desk. There may be times when there is sufficient staff so that two people are scheduled at the same time. Chatting quietly may be one way for staff members to bond, but make sure you don't get so engrossed in conversation that you ignore patrons or give them the impression that they are interrupting you. Try to work as a team, and help each other out. As the old adage says, "Two heads are better than one."

The reference desk might be compared to a concierge desk in a hotel. The concierge/librarian knows just where to look and exactly who to call when helping guests/patrons. It may also be compared to a reception desk, particularly if it is located near the library's main entrance. In either example, the behavior of the librarian at the reference desk will affect a patron's perception of the whole library, and his or her impression of it as a place where you will (or will not) find help. An attentive reference librarian can make a patron feel welcome, assure them that there is someone who can help, and then provide that help in a friendly and professional manner. As Dave Tyckoson so eloquently put it, "The reference librarian is the library's human face."

TWELVE

Telephone Reference Service

Telephone in for what you want, get the formula
you have forgotten, the quotation you can only half
remember, the business address you do not know, the
word you want defined or correctly pronounced, the
place you want located, given you over the telephone.

—"Invitation to Business Men"

THE EPIGRAPH ABOVE illustrates that telephone reference was once promoted to a specific demographic group. The Pottsville Public Library, issuer of the above invitation, and most other libraries heeded the advice offered by Emily Garnett in "Reference Service by Telephone" in that same issue of *Library Journal* that "professional people and business men are more entitled to prompt service by telephone."[1] Garnett thought that "club women" and "school children" should not be encouraged to use telephone reference service since they have the time to come to the library in person!

Today, of course, reference service by telephone is available to anyone with access to a phone. Telephone reference is a convenient service offered to library patrons who, for whatever reason, are not able to visit the library in person. Sometimes callers simply have a question about library hours or policies, and sometimes they want to know the history of the world. Whatever the question, reference service by telephone has its own particular (and often peculiar) characteristics: it's anonymous: you can ask a question that you may well be embarrassed to pose in person. It saves time: you can find out if a book you need is available or if the library subscribes to a certain periodical you'd like to read. When you need to verify a single fact and aren't able to visit the library or need some advice on how to proceed when you do stop in, a competent and courteous librarian on the line can be your best ally. Although today practitioners will tell you that the number of telephone reference questions libraries receive each day is far less than it was before the world was wired, the kinds of queries now heard at the other end of the line are often much more than a request for a fact check. Callers may be on the library's website trying to locate a specific item or execute a search of some kind. They may have been unsuccessfully searching the Web for the answer to a pressing question, or trying to find a phone number and mailing address on a company's or organization's website. Practitioners will also tell you that there are still people without Internet access as well as those unfamiliar with local government, community services, or even the news of the day, and they call the library for help. This practitioner can attest to one of the enduring qualities of telephone reference, and in fact, of any kind of reference work—its infinite variety. Just when you think you've heard it all, a caller may pose a question that stops you in your tracks.

> **Telephone Reference Tip**
>
> It's a good idea to jot down a question when it comes in. Once you put a caller on hold in order to research the question, it is quite possible that you will get distracted by something or someone at your work site, and taking notes will help you avoid having to get back on the phone and ask "Now what was your question?"

Providing reference service by telephone requires the same skills and qualities that are needed at the in-person reference desk—and more. All the components of a standard reference interview (approachability, listening/inquiring, searching, follow-up) should be in evidence when there is a patron at the other end of the line. As might be expected, the lack of visual cues means that the listening/inquiring component is one of utmost importance. On the telephone, all you have is your tone of voice to convey your approachability and interest to a patron. Just as you focus all your attention on the person standing in front of you when you work at the reference desk, you have to concentrate all your attention on the person calling, a process that may be affected by a poor connection, an unfamiliar accent, or background noise.

Time becomes more of a factor in a telephone reference transaction than in an in-person reference encounter, unless, of course, there is a long line in front of the reference desk! Telephone patrons are often multitasking, and most do not like to be kept on hold for an extended period of time. Depending on a library's reference policy, a librarian might have to ask a patron to call back later or ask for a phone number where the patron can be reached later, especially when the query posed will take some time to answer. There is also the kind of telephone reference service (one with which I am very familiar) billed as "quick" or "ready reference," in which the objective is to answer all questions within three to five minutes and where patrons are not called back.

There is another aspect of telephone reference that bears mentioning: citing the source. Citing a source should, of course, be a part of any reference transaction, in-person, online, or on the phone. On the telephone, it is crucial to cite a source lest we give an impression that we are answering questions off the tops of our heads. Telephone reference is not a quiz show, although sometimes when the calls are coming in fast and furious it may seem like one. A recent article in *Reference and User Services Quarterly* by Denise E. Agosto and Holly Anderton, "Whatever Happened to 'Always Cite the Source?' A Study of Source Citing and Ethical Issues Related to Telephone Reference," decried the tendency of reference librarians to neglect to tell callers the source of the information they are relaying to them. In this study, sources were *not* cited in 69 percent of the 125 telephone reference transactions analyzed. Agosto and Anderton also brought to light some disturbing tendencies among the providers of telephone reference service in the study: some of the respondents did not seem to take the questions posed seriously, and in fact Agosto and Anderton refer to their "cavalier attitude." A reference librarian should treat all patrons and their questions with respect, whether those questions are being asked by a person in front of the reference desk or by a voice on the other end of a telephone call. Even if it's a question *you've* heard many times before, that patron is asking it for the *first* time and deserves an appropriate answer relayed in a professional tone of voice.

Telephone Reference Tip

Try smiling as you answer the telephone! Although the caller can't see you, studies have shown that the tone of your voice will be friendlier when you do.

The collection used to answer telephone reference questions depends on the library. Just as some libraries may have a separate telephone reference area, away from the reference desk, there may be a separate reference collection used to support it. In my experience this type of setup, consisting of a good general reference collection of print and electronic resources along with locally developed sources as well as access to the Internet, provides a solid basis for answering telephone reference questions. These resources should be organized in such a way that individual sources can be located quickly and easily. A bank of telephones, or even a single telephone, each one next to a computer with Internet access, surrounded by, or adjacent to, a print collection, is a fairly typical model of a telephone reference service. Wireless headsets and tablet PCs could also allow librarians to go into the stacks in order to answer telephone reference questions.

Just as at the in-person reference desk, there will be some downtime. The time between calls can be spent reading news magazines and other publications, checking news feeds or newspaper websites, or exploring the library's own website and electronic reference sources. And just as at the in-person reference desk, it is very important not to get too engrossed in the page or screen in front of you. A ringing telephone, though, is usually enough to get your attention.

Note

1. Emily Garnett, "Reference Service by Telephone," *Library Journal* 61, no. 21 (December 1, 1936): 911.

THIRTEEN

Online Reference Service

Using electronic means to provide reference assistance
has become part of the lives of most reference
librarians. Answering questions by e-mail, chat, instant
messaging (IM), and text messaging (SMS) is not so
different from answering questions face to face.

—Kay Ann Cassell and Uma Hiremath,
Reference and Information Services in the 21st Century

ONCE UPON A time the telephone was a new technology, and its introduction into reference services caused considerable discussion. When any new form of technology or new type of service is introduced in a library the discussion usually includes questions such as "How will the staff be trained?" "Who will be eligible for this service?" "What are the limits of this service?" "Who will provide this service?" Online reference service, like reference service by telephone, extends reference service beyond the walls of the library's building. What is online reference service? Joan M. Reitz, who refers to it as "digital reference," defines it as

> reference services requested and provided over the Internet, usually via e-mail, instant messaging ("chat"), or Web-based submission forms, usually answered by librarians in the reference department of a library . . . Synonymous with *chat reference, e-reference, online reference* and *virtual reference.*[1]

"Guidelines for Implementing and Maintaining Virtual Reference Services" (see the appendix) includes this definition:

> Virtual reference is reference service initiated electronically where patrons employ computers or other technology to communicate with public services staff without being physically present. Communication channels used frequently in virtual reference include chat, videoconferencing, Voice-over-IP, co-browsing, e-mail, and instant messaging. (2.1)

So instead of asking a question in person at the library or on the telephone, the patron is usually somewhere else (but sometimes actually in the library!) using some form of electronic communication. As you might imagine, these methods of communication have their own particular challenges as well as benefits when used to provide reference service.

For the purpose of this discussion I'd like to focus on the three most widely used forms of online reference: e-mail, chat, and instant messaging (IM).

E-mail Reference

E-mail reference is one of those rare services
that seem to provide very satisfying results for a
relatively small commitment of time and labor.
—Karen G. Schneider, "My Patron Wrote Me a Letter"

E-mail reference is a service that has been offered by most libraries since the 1990s. Using a form on a library's website, a patron submits a question and an e-mail address to which the response can be sent. Other details such as the patron's location, reason for the question (e.g., school assignment, personal interest, etc.), and sources already consulted are often requested on the form as well. An example of an e-mail reference form can be found on *ipl2* (www .ipl2.org) by clicking on "Ask an ipl2 Librarian." This form has been carefully constructed to elicit as much information as possible from the patron (as in any good reference interview), and even explains why each bit of information is requested. For example, opposite the part of the form that asks "How will you use this information?" there is the explanation that "Understanding the context and scope of your information needs helps us to deliver an answer that you will find useful." Opposite "Sources already consulted" on the form is the comment that "Knowing where you've already looked will help us keep from sending you someplace you've already been" (www.ipl.org/div/askus/). By now it should be obvious that asking such questions on an e-mail request form takes the place of the "listening/inquiring" phase of the reference interview. Let's go back to the RUSA "Guidelines for Behavioral Performance of Reference and Information Services Providers" (see the appendix) discussed in chapter 12. These guidelines identified the five components of a successful reference transaction: approachability, interest, listening/inquiring, searching, and follow-up. As previously noted, this version of the RUSA guidelines expanded each of these elements to include the "remote" forms of reference service (telephone, e-mail, chat):

> Under "approachability" we find: "Should provide prominent, jargon-free links to all forms of reference service from the *home page* of the library's web site, and throughout the site wherever research assistance may be sought out. The Web should be used to make reference services easy to find and convenient." (1.8)

So that e-mail request form should be as easy to locate as it is to use. To indicate "interest" the librarian "acknowledges user email questions in a timely manner" (2.7). An automatic message is often generated, such as "your request has been received and you will receive a response in (fill in the blank)." The listening/inquiring stage, as we've seen in the description of the Internet Public Library's e-mail reference form, is carried out by the use of such a form (3.10). As for "searching," the recommendation is that the librarian "uses appropriate technology to help guide patrons through library resources when possible" (4.11). In the case of e-mail reference, this might include providing links to sources or describing how such sources (e.g., a database) can be used. Finally, when it's time for the "follow-up" the librarian "suggests that the patrons visit or call the library when appropriate" (5.9). Sometimes the information requested cannot be relayed by e-mail, and the patron will have to visit the library in person.

Some of the benefits of e-mail reference are

1. The patron can ask the question when it comes to mind (and a computer is available) and not have to deal with busy signals or stand in line.

2. The librarian can work on an e-mail request at a more deliberate pace than what is possible with a queue of callers on the phone or in front of the reference desk
3. The patron will have a written record of the answer (if he or she chooses to print it out!) and won't have to decipher a hastily scribbled note made while calling or search for the call-slip or printout handed out at the reference desk.
4. The librarian doesn't have to decipher an unfamiliar accent, listen to background noise, or keep an eye out for the next person in line.

Some of the challenges of providing e-mail reference service are

1. The patron sending the question may not be able to formulate a question clearly in writing.
2. The librarian may receive e-mail requests that constitute research rather than reference questions.
3. The patron's own e-mail service provider may block out the library's e-mail response, or, if the response is received, the patron might accidentally delete it.
4. The librarian may have to send an additional e-mail (or even two) to clarify what the patron (see no. 1) really needs.

Practitioners will tell you that e-mail reference does indeed, as Karen G. Schneider puts it, require "a relatively small commitment of time and labor." In my experience in a public library, the majority of e-mail requests received concern library policies and resources, local information and death notices and obituaries, all of which can be easily and quickly located. The frequent thank-you messages sent by "e-patrons" bears out the impression that our answers, no matter how "easily and quickly located," are appreciated.

Chat Reference

Like phone and email reference before it, chat
reference offers the opportunity to expand reference
services to others in our user populations. Like most
aspects of digital librarianship, it is "the same but
different"—the same basic concepts are there,
but the applications are different and novel.

—David S. Carter, "Hurry Up and Wait"

You might say that chat reference is to e-mail reference what a telephone call is to a voice mail message. Chat, like a telephone call, is in "real time." There is a person at the other end, and instead of talking to the librarian, they are typing. Unlike e-mail reference, which, like a voice mail message, is static (the message is either written or a voice recording), chat is dynamic, with the give and take of a conversation. Chat requires the use of some special software, and once that is installed all that's left to do is train the staff and establish the hours of service.

As with e-mail reference, chat reference has benefits and challenges. Some of the benefits of chat reference are

> Tammy Bobrowsky, Lynne Beck, and Malaika Grant, "The Chat Reference Interview: Practicalities and Advice," *Reference Librarian* 43, no. 89/90 (2005): 179–91, provides actual chat transcripts, tips from veteran chat reference librarians, and training suggestions.

1. Chat software programs offer transcripts of transactions, offering the patron a record of the information or website addresses provided. These transcripts can also be used for training purposes in the library.
2. Chat reference provides service at the time and place of need.
3. Chat reference allows patrons to ask questions they may feel uncomfortable posing in person.
4. Chat reference service can offer a "teachable moment" when the librarian is able to "push" a web page to the patron or co-browse with them.

Some of the challenges of chat reference are

1. A chat reference service needs to be answered live during the posted hours of service—there is no opportunity to let a question go to voice mail, or, in this case, e-mail. The question will be lost if a response isn't made.
2. Practitioners report that there can be a variety of technical problems associated with chat software programs that can affect the service.
3. Fast, accurate typing is required of both patron and librarian for easily understood transactions.
4. As sometimes happens in telephone reference, patrons often disconnect in the middle of a reference transaction, leaving the librarian to wonder if it was a technical glitch or an unavoidable interruption at the other end.

Chat reference service has been offered by public and academic libraries for more than ten years, and continues as another way to provide reference assistance (and sometimes instruction) to patrons.

IM Reference

IM reference works in much the same way
as do other flavors of reference—just think
of it as a sped-up email transaction.

—Aaron Schmidt and Michael Stephens, "IM Me"

IM (instant messaging) uses free commercial networks, such as Yahoo! Messenger, MSN Instant Messenger, or Google Talk, and has been used for providing reference service for most of this decade. IM reference, or IMR, is a live service, like chat and telephone reference, and presents some of the same challenges in the reference interview. For example, there are no visual or nonverbal clues

David S. Carter, "Hurry Up and Wait: Observations and Tips about the Practice of Chat Reference," *Reference Librarian* 38, no. 79/80 (2003): 113–20. In this article a chat reference veteran offers useful (and often humorous) advice.

from either the librarian or the patron, only the words typed on the screen. As in chat, IM users often use a variety of abbreviations and shortcuts in what they type (e.g., LOL = "laughing out loud" or BTW = "by the way"). Most professionals agree that the librarian should take cues from the patron in deciding how many of these shortcuts to use or how informal to be. The best course of action is to maintain some measure of decorum but, just as you might in an in-person encounter, use humor if appropriate.

Sarah Houghton, "Instant Messaging: Quick and Dirty Reference for Teens and Others," *Public Libraries* 44, no. 4 (July/August 2005): 192–93. This is an account of how one public library instituted an IMR service.

IMR, like telephone, e-mail, and chat reference, offers benefits and challenges. Some of the benefits of IMR are

1. As its name indicates, IMR offers a patron instant access, no line to stand in, no busy signal to endure or telephone tree to navigate.
2. Little staff training is needed, since the software used is not complicated.
3. IMR provides service at the time and point of need.
4. IMR allows patrons to ask questions they may feel uncomfortable posing in person.

Some of the challenges of IM reference are

1. The absence of visual clues, like facial expressions, may make it difficult to determine if the patron understands the librarian's response.
2. Frequent updates may be needed, such as "I'm still looking" or "This may take a few minutes" to assure the patron that the librarian has not disconnected.
3. The nature of IM itself may lead patrons to expect an instantaneous, complete response before a reference interview can be conducted.

Jody Condit Fagan and Christina M. Desai, "Communication Strategies for Instant Messaging and Chat Reference Services," *Reference Librarian* 38, no. 79/80 (2003): 121–55. This article analyzes actual online reference conversations in order to demonstrate how online skills can substitute for the nonverbal communication skills used in face-to-face reference transactions.

4. As sometimes happens in chat and telephone reference, patrons often disconnect in the middle of a reference transaction, leaving the librarian to wonder if it was a technical glitch or an unavoidable interruption at the other end.

Whether the queries are coming in via e-mail, chat, or IM, the goal is the same: to provide reference service. Offering reference service in a variety of formats allows us to reach patrons at their time and point of need and in the way in which they prefer to communicate. Once the technical aspects are dealt with, just remember that there is a *person* with a question at the other end and that goal will be reached.

Note

1. Joan M. Reitz, *Dictionary for Library and Information Science* (Westport, CT: Libraries Unlimited, 2004), 218.

FOURTEEN

Reference Service to Children and Young Adults

Reference work with children is an awesome challenge
that forces the reference librarian to discern a question
amid a complexity of psychological and environmental
variables. The child possesses a question that can be
hidden behind unclear communication, psychological
attitudes and assumptions, and inexperience.

—Linda Ward-Callaghan, "Children's Questions"

S O FAR THE focus has been on the types of reference services (in-person,
telephone, online), and each of those discussions referred to library
patrons in general. One group of patrons, however, requires some special
consideration, as the quotation above illustrates. This is not to say that using
standard reference interviewing techniques with children and young adults
is not appropriate, but rather that there are some additional factors that need
to be taken into consideration when doing so. Children and young adults
constitute a significant portion of the patrons served in public libraries, and
this discussion will reflect that fact.

Among the "complexity of psychological and environmental variables"
to be taken into account when providing reference service to young people
are levels of intellectual, social, and emotional development, vocabulary and
language skills, and familiarity with libraries and information sources. The
realities of the particular library setting, from layout to staffing to policies,
should also be kept in mind.

The reference process is primarily one of communication in which the
librarian attempts to understand the patron's question. Since this process

can become a complex one even when the parties involved are adults who speak the same language, how much more challenging is providing reference assistance to individuals who may not only be just learning to read but to explore and make sense of the world around them? Linda Ward-Callaghan notes that, "because children are often not able to present their requests in the clearest manner, the reference interview becomes the most important step in identifying the details necessary to enable the librarian to provide the best information for each request."[1]

The components of the standard reference interview (approachability, interest, listening/inquiring, searching, and follow-up) need a little fine-tuning when providing reference service to young people. Let's consider each of those elements and how they might be adapted to reference interviews with youthful patrons.

Approachability

For the child, simply approaching a reference desk in the children's department can be a scary proposition. As children are generally less skilled at asking questions, the children's librarian's job is two-fold: to be open (receptive, friendly); and to treat the child's question with respect.

—Kay Bishop and Anthony Salveggi, "Responding to Developmental Stages in Reference Service to Children"

Imagine walking into a place where everyone is taller than you and looking down at you with a less than welcoming expression, or worse, completely ignoring you. Imagine, too, that this is the only place where you can find information for an important school project or a book you would really like to read. Even more so than with adults, the librarian providing reference service to children must convey by body language and a friendly demeanor that the patron is welcome in the library and that there is someone who will listen to their request and help them find what they need. For example, the librarian can come out from behind the desk to talk to the child, or, in the case of a very small child, bend down or kneel until he or she is eye-to-eye with the little one.

Interest

Even though this may be the fifteenth time that a child has asked for information on the state animal, flag, bird, insect, mineral, motto, and so on in the last hour, it is crucial that the librarian demonstrate interest in each child's question. It can be a challenge, particularly if the child is shy or unsure of how to ask a question, but if the librarian communicates "through verbal or non-verbal confirmation, such as nodding of the head or brief comments or questions" ("Guidelines for Behavioral Performance of Reference and Information Service Professionals," 2.5) contact can be established and a "reference relationship" begun.

Listening/Inquiring

A "tone of voice . . . appropriate to the nature of the transaction" (3.2) is a critical component of a reference interview with a child. It is best to avoid the authoritarian approach, and put some friendliness and warmth into your voice. This is always a good idea, whether you are helping an adult or a child, but is especially helpful with a child. Patience is called for, too, since you may need to allow a little extra time for a child to fully express his or her request, or even get to the point. Depending upon their stage of development and language skills, they may have some difficulty in expressing themselves clearly. Factor in the sometimes scary prospect of speaking to an adult and you can easily see why patience and a friendly demeanor are called for. This is the time, too, to refrain from using a lot of library jargon (something to keep in mind with adults as well) and listen more than you speak. Using open-ended questions not only to discover the amount or type of information needed but also to determine the approximate reading level required is yet another aspect of this phase of a reference interview with a child. Linda Ward-Callaghan notes that "the best source in the world is useless to a child

Susan Strong, "Sights, Sounds and Silence in Library Reference Service to Children," *Public Libraries* 43, no. 6 (November/December 2004): 313–14. In this article, an experienced children's librarian takes a look at some important aspects of reference service to elementary school-age children.

who cannot handle the reading level of the material."[2] (She also suggests that when you are unsure of a child's reading ability, "casually [suggest] that the patron might read a few lines to see if the material is too hard or too easy.")[3]

Searching

This is an area that has been the subject of debate among children's librarians for some time: do you show the inquiring child how to find the information requested or do you just provide that information? The literature includes arguments on both sides, but it seems to me that a hybrid approach is best. Provide the information requested but as you are doing so, briefly explain each of the steps taken, for example, "I'm checking the index or catalog, etc. . . ." or, "I'm using this database on our library's website, etc." This "teachable moment" is just one more element of the "value-added" service a reference librarian provides. Some of the advocates of simply telling a child how (or where) to find what they need are operating under the assumption that children only come in to the library for school assignments. Anyone who has actually worked in a public library knows that this is not always the case. Children certainly do read for "fun," and often pursue subjects related to hobbies or other activities like scouting, or simply because they are curious about something. A good reference librarian does not make value judgments on how "serious" a question is and only questions how information will be used in order to determine the best type of material for a particular patron of any age.

> Chuck Ashton, "Chuck's 10 Rules of Children's Reference," *The U*N*A*B*A*S*H*E*D Librarian*, no. 92 (1994): 5. A humorous "Top Ten List" that will ring true for anyone who has ever worked at the reference desk in the children's department.

Follow-Up

To help reinforce the idea of the library (with the services of a reference librarian) as a place to visit with any kind of question, the librarian "asks patrons if their questions have been completely answered" (5.1) and "encourages the patrons to return if they have further questions" (5.2). Although this is something that should be done with all library patrons, it has an added importance when those patrons are young people learning about the world around them.

Up to now the discussion has revolved mainly around young patrons of elementary and middle-school age. What about young people in high school? Just as we would not look at children as "little adults," we should not look at adolescents as "big children." Adolescence is a turbulent time of navigating between childhood and adulthood and finding your place in the world. Reference service to this age group can be a challenge, even though most teens have developed intellectually far beyond their younger counterparts. The raging hormonal storms of this stage of life can even affect behavior in the library.

Recently a joint task force of ALA's Young Adult Library Services Association

> Carol Collier Kuhlthau, "Meeting the Information Needs of Children and Young Adults: Basing Library Media Programs on Developmental States," *Journal of Youth Services in Libraries* 2, no. 1 (Fall 1988): 51–57. This article summarizes the developmental states of young people and relates them to library service.

and Reference and User Services Association created "Guidelines for Library Services to Teens, Ages 12–18" (see the appendix). The section on reference service to teens includes this observation:

> Online information and electronic communication is a way of life for most teens. They have come of age with the Internet, iPods, cable and satellite television, cell phones, etc., and these tools form a seamless part of their everyday life . . . Librarians need to understand how these "digital natives" perceive the world. We need to provide direction, structure, and effective assistance, both when we are asked directly to help as when we are not. Sound and savvy instruction in information literacy and thoughtful design of intuitive and welcoming portals to our virtual libraries are essential allies in serving the needs of teens. (3.0)

Whether you are helping the third-grader in front of you gather information for a science fair project or replying to a teen's text message asking for help with the research for a term paper, keep the fundamentals of reference service and these variables in mind and you will succeed in providing effective reference to patrons of *all* ages.

Notes

1. Linda Ward-Callaghan, "Children's Questions: Reference Interviews with the Young," *Reference Librarian* 2, no. 7/8 (1983): 57.
2. Ibid., 61.
3. Ibid.

FIFTEEN

Reference Service in Special Subjects

Medical, legal and business questions constitute one
of the most specialized, sensitive, and expensive areas
of reference. The eternal realities of birth, death, and
taxes that color all human existence feed inexorably
into an urgent and steady stream of questions in
health, legalities, personal finance, and business.

—Kay Ann Cassell and Uma Hiremath,
Reference and Information Services in the 21st Century

A FTER REVIEWING SOME types of reference service (in-person, telephone, online) and considering some categories of patrons (children and young adults), it's time to explore some of the issues associated with providing reference service in some special subjects, namely, medicine, law, and business. As a reference generalist, I take pride in my ability to answer questions on just about anything from aviation to zydeco, but queries in these subject areas often give me pause.

As Cassell and Hiremath observed, these kinds of questions are not only specialized in their subject content but urgent in their emotional context. Health problems, legal difficulties, and business challenges often cause people to seek out a trusted source for advice and assistance. All too often such help is expensive or difficult to obtain, so many people try to work it out themselves, and go to the library for information. Where the difficulty arises is when that request for information becomes a request for advice. Cassell and Hiremath refer to this as a "handle with care" area of reference work:

The questions are invariably weighty.

The answers are typically multilevel so that some degree of specialized knowledge becomes necessary.

A strong code of ethics must govern the answers.

The resources swallow a significant percentage of reference budgets and require constant updates.

Finally, and most important, reference librarians, who are trained in the art and science of answering questions, must be constantly aware that they are nonspecialists and should calibrate their responses accordingly.[1]

So in these areas reference librarians not only need to know about current resources but also about appropriate ways of responding to questions in these subjects. ALA's Reference and User Services Association provides a set of "Guidelines for Medical, Legal and Business Responses" (see the appendix). Although this revised and updated version (originally issued in 1992) offers a "change in focus of the original intention of the guidelines from one of addressing the needs of non-specialists at general reference desks to one which addresses the needs of both specialists and non-specialists," this discussion will focus on the reference generalist. These revised guidelines also use the term *information services staff* instead of *reference librarian*. The topics covered in these guidelines are the role of the information services staff, sources, information service responses for off-site users, and ethics. What follows is an overview of these areas, and after that, a closer look at medical, legal, and business reference service (or, if you prefer, information service) issues.

Role of Information Services Staff

Here the guidelines recommend that staff members must have the requisite training and subject knowledge to be able to respond to their patrons' questions, stay current in relevant subject areas and, perhaps most important for the reference generalist, refer any questions that may go beyond their own level of expertise or are beyond the scope of their institution's collection or services to the appropriate person or institution. As Cassell and Hiremath noted, these kinds of questions are often fraught with anxiety, fear, and concern. The guidelines counsel us to respect the confidentiality of patrons' requests and use tact and discretion when conducting the reference interview.

Sources

The guidelines recommend that libraries "evaluate and acquire appropriate sources in medical, legal and business subject areas that are current, accurate and accessible to meet the needs of the community served" (2.0.1). In addition, familiarity with public or private agencies or services outside of the library is encouraged. However, "staff may not make recommendations to specific lawyers, legal firms, doctors, other medical care providers or business professionals but may provide access to other information that may help the user identify and locate those resources" (2.3.5).

Information Service Responses
for Off-Site Users

As has been noted in chapter 13, "special care must be taken with off-site requests . . . since . . . text-based communication may need explanation or interpretation" (3.1). Further, such requests for information may need to be answered with an invitation to come to the library in person for reference assistance.

Ethics

The guidelines state that the ALA's Code of Ethics "governs the conduct of all staff members providing the information service" (4.0). The ALA Code of Ethics is an important expression of the principles guiding the profession and is included in the appendix.

The Medical Library Association has also instituted a "Code of Ethics for Health Sciences Librarianship." Its principles are set forth in broad statements that provide health sciences librarians with a basis from which to resolve ethical dilemmas. Among these are the need for health sciences librarians to promote access to health information for all, and to uphold the privacy of clients and the confidentiality of their information requests.

The American Association of Law Libraries issued a statement of "AALL Ethical Principles" in 1999. Among them are the duty to "promote open and effective access to legal and related information" and to "develop service policies that respect confidentiality and privacy." This statement also acknowledges that law librarians have a "duty to avoid the unauthorized practice of law."

Medical Reference

Although the reference interview is an essential element of any type of reference service, it is of utmost importance when the query involves a health or medical topic. Deborah A. Thomas writes that "this process quickly becomes more complicated when the person in need of information is unfamiliar with medical terminology or libraries, is emotionally upset regarding a new diagnosis, or is uncertain about what he/she was told by a physician."[2]

Deborah A. Thomas, "The Consumer Health Reference Interview," *Journal of Hospital Librarianship* 5, no. 2 (2005): 45–56. This article discusses the complexities of conducting a reference interview at a consumer health reference service.

Listening and expressing an interest in a patron's question are critical components of the reference interview, but with this type of query there may be a tendency to get a little too personally involved, as Jana C. Allcock writes:

On occasion, the medical questions posed by the patron may be one that relates to your personal experience. It is important while empathizing to not identify too closely with the patron. It is never appropriate to share a personal experience of an illness with a patron. The focus must stay on finding credible sources of information for the patron.[3]

Just as we have to put aside personal opinions when answering reference questions in subjects that may touch on some of our own "hot button" issues, we have to put aside any personal feelings that might interfere with our responsibility to find the best information we can for the patron with a question about a health or medical matter.

Another element of any reference interview is citing the source of the information provided. In the area of health or medicine this is especially crucial. As reference librarians, we work with the well-chosen, reputable books and online sources in our collections, and we know how to evaluate the credibility of websites. Citing these materials is an essential and should never be omitted from the reference process.

Legal Reference

Just like reference service dealing with health or medical topics, reference service to patrons with questions about the law requires special consideration. Although these questions may not be a matter of life and death, their circumstances may be just as critical. In addition, as Newkirk Barnes writes, there is the possibility of crossing a legal line:

> Reference librarians have to treat legal questions with special care. Generally speaking, reference librarians are not licensed attorneys, so they are not qualified to practice law. Giving legal advice or interpreting the law when one is not qualified to do so may constitute unauthorized practice of law (UPL), a felony in some states.[4]

Barnes goes on to say that "when faced with their users' legal questions, reference librarians have to strike a delicate balance between facilitating access to legal information and actually interpreting it."[5]

In other words, when answering a question related to the law, the reference librarian should concentrate on providing information, or access to it, not on providing advice or even suggestions on how to use that information. In this area, the goal is to supply the information and let the patron decide how to use it. Even providing information can sometimes come dangerously close to providing legal advice. For example, in demonstrating how to use an index, don't use the patron's particular question as an example; instead, use something unrelated and let the patron then decide which terms to use in a search. Keeping the explanation general, concentrating on the "how" rather than on the "what" enables the patron to conduct his or her own research and the librarian to avoid providing legal advice or engaging in UPL.

Charles J. Condon offers "nine strategies for avoiding the unauthorized practice of law." Among them are "avoid lengthy and detailed interviews of the patron"; "prepare research handouts for common research techniques"; "identify and list federal, state and local agencies for referral of patrons"; and "provide directions to access free internet resources." To "avoid lengthy and detailed interviews of the patron" does not mean to dispense with a reference interview entirely; rather, Condon recommends keeping the conversation as general as possible while gathering just enough information to be able to steer the patron to the appropriate resource. By "[preparing] research handouts for common research techniques" librarians can, in effect, create a reference tool that explains the use of standard legal reference sources. When librarians "identify and list federal, state and local agencies for referral of patrons" they can provide relevant referrals

> Charles J. Condon, "How to Avoid the Unauthorized Practice of Law at the Reference Desk," *Legal Reference Services Quarterly* 19, no. 1/2 (2001): 165–79, offers practical advice for librarians providing legal reference service.

for assistance. As has been mentioned elsewhere in this book, an informed referral is often as good as (or even better) than an actual answer. In "providing directions to access free internet resources" librarians can suggest reputable and useful websites supplying legal information.[6]

Business Reference

As do questions related to medical or legal matters, questions related to business matters also require special consideration. According to James Cory Tucker, business reference not only includes fairly simple requests for the address and telephone number of a corporation's headquarters but often fairly complex requests for accounting, banking, or company research:

> Working at the reference desk, library staff must answer questions from multiple disciplines. Among the most difficult to answer are questions related to business. Unless they have had prior experience with business resources, some librarians do not feel comfortable assisting patrons with business inquiries. Due to the fact that business reference can be an intimidating area, developing and implementing a training program is very important.[7]

Business reference questions also have some of the same characteristics of medical or legal queries. For example, questions about taxation or incorporation may require knowledge of the law, and queries about investment or finance may be related to the very survival or demise of a business venture.

As Tucker points out, training is of the utmost importance in this realm of reference. The Business Reference and Services Section (BRASS) of ALA's Reference and User Services Association has made a major effort to keep both business librarians and reference generalists knowledgeable and well-versed in the ways of the business world. To achieve its goal of "[supporting] the needs of business reference librarians and other librarians involved in providing business reference service,"[8] BRASS's Education Committee developed two web guides, "Core Competencies for Business Reference" (www.ala.org/rusa/sections/brass/brassprotools/corecompetencies/corecompetenciesbusiness/) and "Best of the Best Business Web Sites" (www.ala.org/rusa/sections/brass/brassprotools/bestofthebestbus/bestbestbusiness/). The first consists of a set of guides to ten business topics, such as accounting, insurance, and taxation. Each guide includes definitions of basic concepts, key print and online resources for the subject, a glossary of terms, and a list of frequently asked questions. The second lists free websites

> Celia Ross, "Keeping Up with Business Reference," *Journal of Business and Finance Librarianship* 13, no. 3 (2008): 363–70, offers advice for staying current and highlights a number of useful resources.

> Craig Wilkins, "Training Staff for Business Reference," *Journal of Library Administration* 29, no. 1 (2000): 37–45, describes the elements of a business reference training program and includes exercises and training aids.

covering sixteen subject areas, including business ethics, international business, and management information systems and knowledge management.

Familiarity with these tools and a good grasp of reference techniques will help librarians provide reference service in this wide-ranging and ever-changing field.

Notes

1. Kay Ann Cassell and Uma Hiremath, *Reference and Information Services in the 21st Century: An Introduction*, 2nd rev. ed. (New York: Neal-Schuman, 2011), 179.

2. Deborah A. Thomas, "The Consumer Health Reference Interview," *Journal of Hospital Librarianship* 5, no. 2 (2005): 47.

3. Jana C. Allcock, "Helping Public Library Patrons Find Medical Information—The Reference Interview," *Public Library Quarterly* 18, no. 3/4 (2000): 22.

4. Newkirk Barnes, "Handling Legal Questions at the Reference Desk and Beyond," *Electronic Journal of Academic and Special Librarianship* 6, no. 3 (2005): 1.

5. Ibid.

6. Charles J. Condon, "How to Avoid the Unauthorized Practice of Law at the Reference Desk," *Legal Reference Services Quarterly* 19, no. 1/2 (2001): 165–79.

7. James Cory Tucker, "Getting Down to Business: Library Staff Training," *Reference Services Review* 32, no. 3 (2004): 293.

8. Business Reference and Services Section, Reference and User Services Association, "Core Competencies for Business Reference," *Reference and User Services Quarterly* 46, no. 1: 40.

SIXTEEN

Reference Policies

Every library needs a reference policy. Not because it will offer the framework to answer every procedural or philosophical matter that arises, but because it provides a basis for continuity. That is, a policy enables the patron, as well as the librarian, to expect that certain things will be done and likewise, that certain things fall outside the normal expectations of what is known as reference service.

—Bernard Vavrek, "After the Guidelines and Reference Policy"

R EFERENCE POLICIES DO not, as Vavrek observes in the epigraph, address every eventuality; rather, they clarify and even codify the elements of reference service in a particular library. They are not so much rulebooks, however, as they are outlines of services and their parameters (i.e., what services will be provided, who will provide them, to whom will they be provided).

This chapter examines the basic components of reference policies and discusses some of the reasons for having (and using) them. Often standards (e.g., of services, collections, and staff behavior) are part of reference policies, and they will be considered in chapter 17. Evaluations measure, among other things, how well standards are being met, and they will be addressed in chapter 18.

In general, a reference policy should begin with a statement of purpose; for example, "The purpose of the Reference Services Manual is to state guidelines for providing reference service in order to insure a uniform standard of service of the highest possible quality consistent with available resources."[1] This sentence clearly states the purpose of this institution's reference policy—to furnish the staff with guidelines for providing reference service. Such a statement can be particularly useful when there is a large reference staff or when a library has multiple locations at which reference service is provided. Having guidelines ensures that everyone involved in the reference process (patrons as well as staff) is on the same page. Notice, too, that this statement incorporates an institutional goal—to offer the best possible reference service using the resources at hand.

In "Reference Service Policies," *Reference Services Review* 13, no. 2 (Summer 1985): 79–82, Janet Easley lists five reasons for a reference policy: "A reference service policy establishes standards of service; assists in training new staff members; establishes levels of service to users, including limits of service; establishes priorities of service; and describes practical procedures that answer practical questions" (80).

In 1991 the board of ALA's Reference and Adult Services Division, now known as the Reference and User Services Association, asked the Management of Reference Services Committee (now the Management of Reference Committee) of the Management and Operation of Public Services Section, now the Reference Services Section (RSS), to draft an outline for use by reference librarians and others in academic, public, and special libraries who want to develop reference or information service policy manuals. The author was a member of that committee, which designed this outline to supplement, not supplant, existing reference guidelines and standards (many of these are listed in the appendix).

"Information Services Policy Manual: An Outline" was published in the Winter 1994 issue of the *Reference Quarterly* (no. 2, pp. 165–72). It consists of five main sections: mission statement; organizational structure for reference services; services and service philosophy; personnel; reference collection(s) policy.

Mission Statement

Here, as in the example previously cited, is a recommendation for beginning a reference policy with a statement of basic service goals. These should also include a statement of professional ethics, a description of the library's clientele, and a statement affirming that reference services are "nondiscriminatory on the basis of age, race, sexual preference, or disability" (A.4).

Organizational Structure for Reference Service

This is where organizational charts for the library as well as the reference department reside. The former should show the "inter-relationships between the reference department and other library units" (II A), and the latter should illustrate "the functions and inter-relationships of all personnel within the reference department" (II B).

Services and Service Philosophy

This is the heart of any reference policy: From a general statement of service philosophy which includes statements on the provision, level, and evaluation of reference service, it expands to describe the various kinds of reference services offered (i.e., at reference desks, by telephone, via e-mail or written correspondence, by appointment, etc.); the parameters of each (i.e., time limits, length and depth of questions, etc.); the type of statistics kept, and the manner in which each service is evaluated. Other topics to be addressed in this section include electronic reference service to remote users; referrals and cooperative reference; user education; document delivery and services to patrons with special needs; and services in special subjects.

Personnel

The responsibilities of the reference staff are laid out here, as are professional development and training (including new staff orientation) and expectations for their continuing education and professional activities. The criteria used for the evaluation of individual staff members is also outlined here.

Reference Collection(s) Policy

Beginning with a statement of the purpose and scope of the policy, this section should include a definition of reference materials; guidelines for their selection (including subject coverage and appropriate formats) and management (who orders what, how often the collection is weeded and by whom, etc.), and access guidelines (physical arrangement of the collection, restrictions on its use, security procedures, etc.).

By now it should be fairly obvious that a reference policy is a useful document to have on hand. William A. Katz set out the fundamental reasons for having a reference policy:

> Bill Katz and Anne Clifford, eds., *Reference and Online Services Handbook: Guidelines, Policies and Procedures for Libraries* (New York: Neal-Schuman, 1982); and Bill Katz, ed., *Reference and Online Services Handbook: Guidelines, Policies, and Procedures for Libraries, Volume II* (New York: Neal Schuman, 1986) offer numerous examples of policies as well as general guidelines and discussions of related issues.

1. The drafting or modification of a policy requires some appreciation of the overall goals, purpose, and direction of reference services. The systematic analysis of service given, or not given, helps to formulate these necessary objectives.

2. Standards are established, not only for service but also for such things as building the collection, handling of interlibrary loan materials, and preparation of correspondence.

3. A better view of the audience served (or not served) is achieved by considering objectives and standards. Obviously, neither can be analyzed without a careful study of library patrons.

4. Levels of service must be considered, that is, just how much assistance is to be given to help the user in finding information or in actually finding the information for the user.

5. Without a view of the world beyond the scope of the reference desk, services may become less than ambitious, locked more into routine and daily expediency than addressed to long-range needs of the individual and community the library hopes to serve.

6. Policy statements are developed to resolve controversies such as why the microforms staff cannot do all the threading of film readers or why the advance notice of a class assignment is necessary.

7. The policy serves as a touchstone of continuity for new staff and helps refresh the memory of veterans who may need a guide for rarely occurring problems.

8. Since there usually are not enough staff members for ideal service, the statement establishes priorities in the hierarchy of services.

9. And this leads to probably the most useful aspect of the policy statement: It serves to clarify, if not always answer, nagging queries about the limits of service that the librarian faces daily.[2]

A reference policy is a systematic way to describe services offered and a reminder of the philosophy and goals that inform and support them. It is useful in staff training (and retraining) and provides a starting point from which to launch new services or fine-tune existing ones.

Notes

1. "Reference Services Manual," University of Massachusetts at Amherst, ERIC Document, ED 200 211, p. 1.

2. William A. Katz, *Introduction to Reference Work*, vol. 2, *Reference Services and Processes*, 8th ed. (New York: McGraw-Hill, 2002), 185.

SEVENTEEN

Reference Standards

We provide the highest level of service to all library users
through appropriate and usefully organized resources;
equitable service policies; equitable access; and accurate,
unbiased, and courteous responses to all requests.

—Article I, Code of Ethics of the American Library Association

T HE STATEMENT ABOVE affirms a standard toward which all librarians should aim in the practice of their profession. Its last few words, "accurate, unbiased and courteous responses to all requests," are particularly germane to those in the realm of reference. In this chapter the focus is on professional and personal reference standards. Professional standards are service guidelines that have been established by individual institutions as well as professional organizations: in the former sometimes as part of a reference policy, and in the latter, as a statement adopted by (and for) its membership. By personal standards I mean the commitment made by a reference librarian to a continuous improvement of skills and the pursuit of lifelong learning.

Professional Standards

The Reference and User Services Association
is responsible for stimulating and supporting
excellence in . . . the provision of reference and
information services . . . in every type of library.

—"About RUSA" (www.ala.org/rusa/about/)

One way to support excellence is to create standards against which services can be measured. Since the ALA bylaws allow only divisions whose focus is a type of *library* (e.g., the Public Library Association) to adopt standards, RUSA, as a division that concentrates on a type of library *activity* (reference), may only compile guidelines. In this discussion *standards* and *guidelines* are used interchangeably.

As of this writing, committees of the RUSA membership have produced nine sets of guidelines under the heading of "Reference/Information Services." They are

- "New Definition of Reference" (2008)
- "Guidelines for Behavioral Performance of Reference and Information Services Providers" (2004)
- "Guidelines for Cooperative Reference Services" (2006)
- "Guidelines for Implementing and Maintaining Virtual Reference Services" (2010)
- "Guidelines for Information Services" (2000)
- "Guidelines for Liaison Work in Managing Collections and Services" (2010)
- "Guidelines for Medical, Legal, and Business Responses" (2001)
- "Guidelines for Preparation of a Bibliography" (2010)
- "Professional Competencies for Reference and User Services Librarians" (2003)

Some of these have already been considered ("definition of reference" in the introduction; "behavioral guidelines" in chapter 10; "virtual reference services" in chapter 13; and "medical, legal and business responses" in chapter 15); all of them may be found in the appendix.

The last RUSA guideline listed above, "Professional Competencies for Reference and User Services Librarians," was intended to "provide librarians, libraries, and information centers with a model statement of competencies essential for successful reference . . . librarians" (introduction). It incorporates the "Guidelines for Behavioral Performance of Reference and Information Services Providers" to offer a detailed description of the skills essential for excellence in reference service. Each section includes a goal followed by strategies that may be used to realize it.

> **A reference reality check:** in "First Impressions and Rethinking Restroom Questions," *Reference and User Services Quarterly* 49, no. 1 (2009): 4–6, Lorraine J. Pellack reminds us that *every* patron's question is important.

After providing definitions of "reference and user services librarians" and "competencies" the guidelines enumerate these areas:

- Access
- Knowledge Base
- Marketing/Awareness/Informing
- Collaboration
- Evaluation and Assessment of Resources and Services

Under each of these headings there is an explanatory paragraph listing the competencies covered followed by several subheadings under which goals and strategies are listed. The importance of communication skills in providing reference service has been previously addressed, particularly in the discussion on the reference interview (chapter 10). Here again communication skills are stressed: Under "Access" the first subheading is "Responsiveness," and the goal set forth is "A librarian provides services that are responsive to user needs." Among the strategies recommended are demonstrating approachability, showing an interest in patrons and their requests, and using active listening techniques in all interactions at the reference service point. In the section of the guidelines entitled "Collaboration," not only is the importance of working closely with colleagues emphasized, but under the subheading of "Relationship with users" the goal stated is "A librarian treats the user as a collaborator and partner in the information seeking process." Here again there is a reference to the behavioral guidelines, specifically, the recommendation for listening/inquiring, searching, and follow-up.

Virginia Massey-Burzio, "Education and Experience: or, the MLS Is Not Enough," in "Reference Librarian of the Future," *Reference Services Review* 19 (Spring 1991): 72–74. Although written nearly twenty years ago, the author's observations still ring true and constitute sound advice.

Another portion of these guidelines is entitled "Knowledge Base," under which "the areas of knowledge essential for reference and user services librarians" are listed. A key statement in this section reads: "Core knowledge is acquired as part of basic professional education. However, knowledge must be continuously updated." To that end, the goals and strategies presented are those concerned with keeping the individual librarian current.

Personal Standards

As the guidelines above have stated so succinctly, "knowledge must be continuously updated." Personal experience bears this out: if I had stopped learning upon the completion of my professional degree, I would be ill-equipped to handle much of what I encounter in a typical reference workday. Among the many strategies for keeping current suggested by the guidelines, some of my favorite ones are regular attendance at local and national library conferences; listening, reading, and viewing a variety of media; and active participation in professional organizations.

In addition to a commitment to lifelong learning, a reference librarian should also aspire to a *personal* standard of excellence. Certainly some days at the reference desk will be more challenging than others, but, it is hoped, "good" days will outnumber the "bad" ones. Whatever the day may bring, a genuine commitment to both serve and stay engaged in the field will go a long way.

Diane Zabel, ed., *Reference Reborn: Breathing New Life into Public Services Librarianship* (Santa Barbara, CA: Libraries Unlimited, 2011), is a collection of thirty-three essays that address the challenges faced by today's reference practitioners.

One way to stay engaged is to attend conferences where interactions with colleagues and presentations by innovators and leaders can energize as well as inform. At the 2008 ALA Annual Conference in Anaheim, the RUSA Presidents Program, "Quality Service in an Impersonal World," offered much in the way of inspiration. One of the most dynamic presenters was Marie L. Radford of Rutgers University, whose research interests include the interpersonal communication aspects of reference, nonverbal communication, and the evaluation of virtual reference. The Winter 2008 (vol. 48, no. 2, pp. 110–15) issue of *Reference and User Services Quarterly* includes an editorial she was asked to write, based, in part, on that presentation. Entitled "A Personal Choice: Reference Service Excellence," it contains these insightful and encouraging words: "Excellent service frequently comes to the personal choices we make to learn, to embrace change, to push into uncharted cyber-territory, to choose to find positive approaches to even the most problematic people."[1]

Note

1. Marie L. Radford, "A Personal Choice: Reference Service Excellence," *Reference and User Services Quarterly* 48, no. 2 (2008): 115.

EIGHTEEN

Reference Evaluation

In general evaluation of reference and information
services relates to the quality of the service, even
when librarians or users cannot easily measure
quality in quantitative or monetary terms.
Improving the quality of service . . . is the objective
of the evaluation of reference services.

—Bryce Allen, "Evaluation of Reference Services"

IN ORDER TO "improve the quality of service," the first step is finding out
what works—and what doesn't. Evaluation is a way to gather the information needed to improve existing services as well as initiate new ones. Regular
appraisals help keep reference services viable and relevant. This chapter provides an overview of reference evaluation and discusses some of the methods
that may be used.

"Measuring and Assessing Reference Services and Resources: A Guide"
is a comprehensive document that "offers an expansive definition of reference service, assessment planning advice, and measurement tools to assist
managers evaluating reference services and resources" (http://connect.ala
.org/node/97245/). Prepared by the RUSA/RSS Evaluation of Reference and
User Services Committee, it includes a list of four key books on reference
service assessment and is divided into four main parts: "Definition of Reference," "Planning Reference Assessment," "Measuring and Assessing Reference
Transactions, Services," and "Measuring and Assessing Reference Resources—
Use, Usability, and Collection Assessment."

Definition of Reference

Before launching an evaluation it is necessary to know exactly *what* is being evaluated! In 2008 the RUSA board of directors approved definitions of reference transactions and reference work. Reference transactions were defined as "information consultations in which library staff recommend, interpret, evaluate, and/or use information resources to help others meet particular information needs."

Reference work was described as "reference transactions and other activities that involve the creation, management, and assessment of information or research resources, tools, and services."

Planning Reference Assessment

This section offers advice and a series of questions to consider before beginning an evaluation. Among them are

- What questions are you trying to answer?
- What performance or quality standards will you use to measure your success?
- How are you going to use the data generated?
- What measurements will you need to generate the data that you want?

Measuring and Assessing Reference Transactions and Services

Here the focus is on the quantitative and qualitative assessment of reference services as well as reference transactions. Links to selected measurement tools and bibliographic references are provided. Topics covered include the analysis of reference transactions, cost-benefit analysis, and quality analysis, specifically, patron needs and satisfaction.

Measuring and Assessing Reference Resources— Use, Usability, and Collection Assessment

In this section the importance of assessing both print and electronic reference collections is highlighted with accompanying links to selected measurement tools and bibliographic references.

So what are some typical forms of reference evaluation? Evaluation methods may vary from the simplest tallies of the number of reference transactions handled and recorded by hash marks on a piece of paper to detailed online questionnaires that rate patron satisfaction.

As the discussion so far has indicated, some of the most frequent subjects for reference evaluation have been reference services, reference collections, and reference staff. Here are some of the forms of evaluations used in assessing each.

Reference Services

Quantitative as well as qualitative measures may be used to evaluate reference services. For example, the number of questions answered in a given time period may be counted (quantitative) or how well they were answered (qualitative) may be assessed (correct answer, patron is satisfied, etc.). Knowing when the most reference transactions occur will indicate when to schedule staff, and may also be used in decisions about staffing levels. Knowing how reference questions are answered may reveal subject areas with which staff members may not be as familiar as they should, and thus indicate where training is needed. Knowing how patrons perceive the reference service they receive may also indicate where staff training, retraining, or "attitude adjustment" is called for.

While quantitative evaluation may produce a "snapshot" of reference activity in a particular time period at a particular service point (for example, how many reference transactions were conducted), it may not provide the "big picture," that is, not only *how many* transactions but *how* they were handled—were patrons satisfied with the outcome; were they (patrons) welcomed, listened to, treated with respect, and so on. This is the kind of information that a qualitative evaluation is intended to yield. Acquiring this kind of information may require a little more than checkmarks on a form. It need not be a lengthy personal interview with each patron; however, there should be a method for gathering patron responses/reactions. One such method was discussed by Jonathan Miller in "Quick and Easy Reference Evaluation: Gathering Users' and Providers' Perspectives."[1] In it, Miller noted that most libraries count the number of reference transactions handled in a given time period. He also observed that "it is more difficult to measure the quality of the reference service we provide."[2] He described an evaluation conducted at several academic libraries in Pittsburgh in which "the challenge . . . was to combine the power of evaluations from both sides of the reference desk."[3] In a short questionnaire the survey asked patrons if they got the information needed, had a better understanding of how to find and evaluate information, and if they were satisfied with the reference transaction. The same questions were also posed to reference providers. A two-part form was used, with one part handed to the patron and one kept by the reference provider. A control number on each part ensured that the responses could be matched up when the data were analyzed.

Another form of reference service evaluation is WOREP, the Wisconsin Ohio Reference Evaluation Program developed in 1983 by Charles Bunge and Marjorie Murfin. This survey also consists of a two-part form in which both the patron and the reference librarian are questioned about the transaction. It is considerably longer than the previous example, and there are versions available for both public and academic libraries. More information may be found at https://worrep.library.kent.edu.

Reference Collections

Just as regular evaluations help keep reference services viable and relevant, regular assessments of reference collections ensure that the sources used to provide reference service are useful and up-to-date. Kay Ann Cassell and Uma Hiremath note that

> collections should be assessed on a regular basis to ascertain whether the materials meet the needs of the users and whether the selections are worth the cost. This is a two-pronged process that involves both determining gaps in the existing collection and evaluating the quality of available resources.[4]

There are a variety of methods that may be used to assess or evaluate a reference collection. Christopher W. Nolan discusses them in a chapter in his book on reference collections. He writes that "any reference collection must be regularly evaluated to ensure that it is still performing its reference functions successfully. Several evaluation methods, both formal and informal, can be used to ascertain its quality."[5] Informal methods might involve obtaining feedback from those who use the reference collection, whether they are

> Jo Bell Whitlach, *Evaluating Reference Service: A Practical Guide* (Chicago: American Library Association, 2000), is a comprehensive guide to the literature of reference evaluation.

library patrons or members of the reference staff. For example, Nolan points out that "patrons frequently speak with reference staff about what they have found that works well, what they would like to find but could not locate, and what they found that did not suit their needs."[6] He also notes that

> reference staff are also users of the collection, and their feedback is very useful in evaluating the collection. Every time a librarian attempts to solve a user query provides an opportunity to observe whether the reference collection offers a solution. Over time, staff will usually develop a feeling that certain sources work well for reference service and others rarely seem to be needed.[7]

However, Nolan offers a caveat about the use of feedback in evaluating a reference collection:

> Note that feedback from library users and staff about the sources that they found helpful tends to give the most information about sources that were used and very little about sources that were not consulted. Managers of reference collections can learn from this feedback that some sources are valuable and should be kept in the collection, but there is almost no way of knowing whether many, or even most, of the items on the shelf (or available on work stations) are ever used by anyone. Use studies . . . attempt to fill this gap in knowledge.[8]

Use studies may involve techniques as simple as keeping track of which reference books are left on tables at the end of the day (presumably they have been used). They may also entail more sophisticated methods such as gathering use statistics provided by database vendors or collecting them with homegrown computer applications. Mary Biggs reviewed a variety of ways to conduct usage studies. She "summarize[d] the principal research methods employed, consider[ed] their applicability, and set forth suggestions for multi-faceted explorations of reference collection use."[9]

David A. Tyckoson, "Wrong Questions, Wrong Answers: Behavioral vs. Factual Evaluation of Reference Services," *Reference Librarian* 17, no. 38 (1992): 151–73, proposes reference evaluation based on behavioral factors and the accountability of reference librarians.

Another way to evaluate or assess a reference collection is to compare it to standard reference lists such as *Reference Sources for Small and Medium-Sized Libraries* (ALA), *Recommended Reference Books for Small and Medium-Sized Libraries and Media Centers* (Libraries Unlimited), and *Guide to Reference* (ALA).

When an evaluation reveals that there are gaps of some type, that is, in subjects, in a reference collection, it's time to look for some new titles. In addition to the retrospective lists mentioned above, reviews are another source of selection ideas. For new reference titles, the most frequently used publications are the "Reference Books Bulletin" of ALA's *Booklist*, the *Reference and User Services Quarterly* (RUSA), *Library Journal* and *School Library Journal* (both published by Media Source, Inc.), and *Choice* (ALA's Association of College and Research Libraries). All of these publications cover electronic as well as print reference sources, some combining print and electronic reviews, others featuring special columns of reviews of electronic reference resources. In addition, *Library Journal* compiles an annual list of "Best Reference Sources" and *American Libraries* (ALA) publishes the annual list of "Outstanding Reference Sources" created by the Outstanding Reference Sources Committee of ALA/RUSA's Collection Organization Development and Evaluation Section. Finally, the *American Reference Books Annual* is published each year by Libraries Unlimited and supplies reviews of the new print and electronic reference works published in the United States and Canada.

When an evaluation reveals gaps in a collection, reviews and retrospective lists are consulted for titles to add. When an evaluation reveals old or outdated

sources it's time to subtract. Cassell and Hiremath offer these criteria for weeding or "deselecting" reference materials:

- The content is no longer up-to-date or accurate.
- A new edition is available.
- The reference work is seldom used.
- The information is duplicated in another reference work.
- The book is worn out.[10]

They note that some subject areas require more frequent weeding than others.
Generally speaking, there is less need for weeding reference sources covering
the humanities than for those covering the sciences.

Reference Staff

Reference services staff may be regularly evaluated as library employees by
means of performance evaluations administered by the managers or supervi-
sors in their particular institution. This section is not concerned with that
kind of evaluation; rather, it discusses *personal* evaluation, or *self*-evaluation
of the reference staff.

   As reference librarians we should keep informed about current events and
our own library's collections and services (and those of nearby institutions); we
also need to monitor our own reference practice. By reference practice I mean
all that we do as reference librarians: answer reference questions, help patrons
formulate a search, build and maintain ref-
erence collections, interact with patrons and
coworkers, and so on. We must make an
effort to keep our reference skills sharp, our
attitude positive, and our enthusiasm high.

   Keeping our reference skills sharp may
be the easiest of these to accomplish since
continuing education opportunities are
plentiful, from in-house training to web-
based instruction and webinars to local
workshops and professional conferences.

Sandra Naiman, "The
Unexamined Interview Is Not
Worth Having," *Reference
Librarian* 6, no. 19 (1987): 31–46.
This article is a thoughtful look
at the reference interview and
the skills and characteristics that
make good reference librarians.

If we find, upon reflection, that there is a particular type of reference situation we have difficulty with or a subject with which we are not as familiar as

we would like to be, it is up to us to seek out some appropriate training or retraining. We need to know our reference strengths and weaknesses and work on maintaining the former and improving the latter.

Maintaining a positive attitude and a high (or at least consistent) level of enthusiasm requires more than release time and a registration fee; they require some honest self-examination or even some contemplation. By a positive attitude I don't mean a Pollyannaish outlook, and by enthusiasm I don't mean relentless rah-rah's. Instead I'm referring to some self-awareness as well as a realistic view of the particular library in which you work. Know your own abilities and skills as well as the institutional culture at your workplace. Focus on the patrons you serve and know that you do make a difference in their lives. Enjoy being part of a profession where every day you have the ability and opportunity to learn about anything and everything and share it with your patrons and colleagues. Stay involved and contribute your time and talent to local and national professional organizations.

Notes

1. Jonathan Miller, "Quick and Easy Reference Evaluation: Gathering Users' and Providers' Perspectives," *Reference and User Services Quarterly* 47, no. 3 (Spring 2008): 218–22.
2. Ibid., 219.
3. Ibid.
4. Kay Ann Cassell and Uma Hiremath, *Reference and Information Services in the 21st Century: An Introduction*, 2nd rev. ed. (New York: Neal-Schuman, 2011), 344.
5. Christopher W. Nolan, *Managing the Reference Collection* (Chicago: American Library Association, 1999), 153.
6. Ibid., 153–54.
7. Ibid., 154.
8. Ibid., 155.
9. Mary Biggs, "Discovering How Information Seekers Seek: Methods of Measuring Reference Collection Use," *Reference Librarian* 13, no. 29 (1990): 104.
10. Cassell and Hiremath, *Reference and Information Services in the 21st Century*, 345.

APPENDIX
ALA DOCUMENTS

ALA's Core Competencies of Librarianship. www.ala.org/educationcareers/careers/corecomp/corecompetences/

Code of Ethics of the American Library Association. www.ifmanual.org/codeethics/

Competencies for Librarians Serving Children in Public Libraries. www.ala.org/alsc/edcareeers/alsccorecomps/

Guidelines for Behavioral Performance of Reference and Information Services Professionals. www.ala.org/rusa/resources/guidelines/guidelinesbehavioral/

Guidelines for Implementing and Maintaining Virtual Reference Services. www.ala.org/rusa/resources/guidelines/

Guidelines for Information Services. www.ala.org/rusa/resources/guidelines/guidelinesinformation/

Guidelines for Library Services to Teens, Ages 12–18. www.ala.org/rusa/resources/guidelines/guidelinesteens/

Guidelines for Medical, Legal, and Business Responses. www.ala.org/rusa/resources/guidelines/guidelinesmedical/

New Definition of Reference. www.ala.org/rusa/resources/guidelines/definitionsreference/

Professional Competencies for Reference and User Services Librarians. www.ala.org/rusa/resources/guidelines/professional/

YALSA's Competencies for Librarians Serving Youth: Young Adults Deserve the Best. www.ala.org/yalsa/guidelines/yacompetencies2010/

BIBLIOGRAPHY

AALL Ethical Principles. American Association of Law Libraries. www.aallnet.org/about/ policy_ethics.asp. The formal statement of the principles under which law librarians and legal information professionals practice.

Agosto, Denise E., and Holly Anderton. "Whatever Happened to 'Always Cite the Source'? A Study of Source Citing and Ethical Issues Related to Telephone Reference." *Reference and User Services Quarterly* 47, no. 1 (2007): 44–54. A wake-up call for librarians who provide telephone reference service that includes suggestions for improvement.

Allcock, Jana C. "Helping Public Library Patrons Find Medical Information—The Reference Interview." *Public Library Quarterly* 18, no. 3/4 (2000): 21–27. Discusses the reference interview in the context of providing health information to public library patrons and includes techniques for avoiding personal liability in doing so.

Allen, Bryce. "Evaluation of Reference Services." In *Reference and Information Services: An Introduction*, 3rd ed., ed. Richard E. Bopp and Linda C. Smith, 245–63. Englewood, CO: Libraries Unlimited, 2001. An overview of the issues involved, and techniques used, in the evaluation of reference services.

American Library Association, *Reference Books Bulletin* Editorial Board. *Purchasing an Encyclopedia: 12 Points to Consider.* Chicago: American Library Association, 1996. Enumerates a dozen factors to be taken into account when choosing an encyclopedia.

American Reference Books Annual. Littleton, CO: Libraries Unlimited, 1970–. Comprehensive source of reference reviews available in print and online at http://arbaonline.com.

Ashton, Chuck. "Chuck's Ten Rules of Children's Reference." *The U*A*B*A*S*H*E*D™ Librarian* 92 (1994): 5. Humorous but nonetheless sound advice for anyone engaged in reference service to children.

Barnes, Newkirk. "Handling Legal Questions at the Reference Desk and Beyond." *Electronic Journal of Academic and Special Librarianship* 6, no. 3 (2005). Offers practical advice for answering legal reference questions.

"Best Free Reference Web Sites: Twelfth Annual List." *Reference and User Services Quarterly* 50, no. 1 (2010): 19–24. An annual guide to the best reference sites on the Web compiled by the MARS Best Free Reference Websites Committee of RUSA.

"Best of the Best Business Web Sites." www.ala.org/rusa/sections/brass/brassprotools/ bestofthebestbus/bestbestbusiness/. A list of free websites covering sixteen business subjects, including business ethics, knowledge management, and more.

Biggs, Mary. "Discovering How Information Seekers Seek: Methods of Measuring Reference Collection Use." *Reference Librarian* 13, no. 29 (1990): 103–17. Reviews methods for assessing the use of reference collections and recommends ways to conduct usage studies.

Bishop, Kay, and Anthony Salveggi. "Responding to Developmental Stages in Reference Service to Children." *Public Libraries* 40, no. 6 (2001): 354–58. Discusses how reference librarians can better serve young patrons.

Bobrowsky, Tammy, Lynne Beck, and Malaika Grant. "The Chat Reference Interview: Practicalities and Advice." *Reference Librarian* 43, no. 89/90 (2005): 179–91. Using actual chat transcripts, veterans of the chat reference service at the University of Minnesota–Twin Cities offer tips and training ideas.

Bopp, Richard E., and Linda C. Smith, eds. *Reference and Information Services: An Introduction.* 4th ed. Santa Barbara, CA: Libraries Unlimited, 2011. The latest edition of a widely used textbook that includes new chapter contributors and incorporates new ideas and methods of providing reference service.

Bridgewater, Rachel, and Meryl B. Cole. *Instant Messaging Reference: A Practical Guide.* Oxford: Chandos, 2009. A comprehensive guide to instant messaging as a reference tool that goes beyond the basics.

Brown, Stephanie Willen. "The Reference Interview: Theories and Practice." *Library Philosophy and Practice* 10, no. 1 (2008): 1–8. Covers the basic elements of the reference interview and cites key works in the professional literature.

Brown, Yvette. "From the Reference Desk to the Jailhouse: Unauthorized Practice of Law and Librarians." *Legal Reference Services Quarterly* 13, no. 4 (1994): 31–45. Offers librarians suggestions and strategies for avoiding UPL, or the unauthorized practice of law.

Carter, David S. "Hurry Up and Wait: Observations and Tips about the Practice of Chat Reference." *Reference Librarian* 38, no. 79/80 (2003): 113–20. Practical advice from a chat reference veteran.

Cassell, Kay Ann, and Uma Hiremath. *Reference and Information Services in the 21st Century: An Introduction.* 2nd rev. ed. New York: Neal-Schuman, 2011. The best reference textbook currently available features a companion website at www.neal-schuman.com/ reference21st/2nd/.

Code of Ethics for Health Sciences Librarianship. Medical Library Association. www.mlanet .org/about/ethics.html. A formal statement of the principles under which health sciences librarians practice.

Condon, Charles J. "How to Avoid the Unauthorized Practice of Law at the Reference Desk." *Legal Reference Services Quarterly* 19, no. 1/2 (2001): 165–79. Discusses the role of law librarians as information providers.

"Core Competencies for Business Reference." www.ala.org/rusa/sections/brass/brassprotools/corecompetencies/corecompetenciesbusiness/. Describes the ten core competencies guides developed and maintained by the Education Committee of the Business Reference and Services Section of RUSA.

Dervin, Brenda, and Patricia Dewdney. "Neutral Questioning: A New Approach to the Reference Interview." *Reference Quarterly* 25, no. 4 (1986): 506–13. Looks at a reference interview strategy based on sense-making methodology in which a question is approached from the patron's, rather than the librarian's, point of view.

Dewdney, Patricia, and Gillian Michell. "Oranges and Peaches: Understanding Communication Accidents in the Reference Interview." *Reference Quarterly* 35, no. 4 (1996): 520–36. A linguistic analysis of "ill-formed" questions that result in communication accidents at the reference desk.

Dewdney, Patricia, and Catherine Sheldrick Ross. "Flying a Light Aircraft: Reference Service Evaluation from a User's Viewpoint." *Reference Quarterly* 34, no. 2 (1994): 217–30. When MLIS students reported on their experiences asking reference questions in a library, an analysis of their accounts revealed areas for improvement and suggested appropriate remedies.

Dilevko, Juris, and Elizabeth Dolan. "Reference Work and the Value of Reading Newspapers: An Unobtrusive Study of Telephone Reference Service." *Reference and User Services Quarterly* 39, no. 1 (1994): 71–81. Discusses the importance of keeping up with current issues and emerging trends by regular perusal of newspapers and periodicals.

Easley, Janet. "Reference Service Policies." *Reference Services Review* 13, no. 2 (1985): 79–82. Presents five arguments for instituting a policy for reference services.

East, John W. "The Rolls Royce of the Library Reference Collection: The Subject Encyclopedia in the Age of Wikipedia." *Reference and User Services Quarterly* 50, no. 2 (2010): 162–69. Reviews the development of the subject encyclopedia and reflects on its future as a reference source.

Fagan, Jody Condit, and Christina M. Desai. "Communication Strategies for Instant Messaging and Chat Reference Services." *Reference Librarian* 38, no. 79/80 (2003): 121–55. Analyzes online reference conversations in order to demonstrate how online skills can substitute for the nonverbal cues found in face-to-face reference interviews.

Fisher, Donna M. "The Importance of Being Ear-Nest." *Information Outlook* 9, no. 10 (2005): 39. Emphasizes the importance of listening in reference work.

Garnett, Emily. "Reference Service by Telephone." *Library Journal* 61, no. 21 (December 1, 1936): 909–11. One of the earliest, if not the earliest, articles on telephone reference in library literature.

Gifford, Florence M. "Telephone Reference Services." *Wilson Library Bulletin* 17, no. 8 (April 1943): 630–32. Advice on providing telephone reference service circa 1943 still rings true.

Goulding, Mary. "Real Librarians Don't Play Jeopardy." *Illinois Libraries* 77, no. 2 (1991): 140–46. Looks at a reference training method that emphasizes starting from the question rather than the answer or a reference source.

Grathwohl, Casper. "Wikipedia Comes of Age." *Chronicle Review*, January 7, 2011. http://chronicle.com/article/Wikipedia-Comes-of-Age/125899/. Considers the role of *Wikipedia* "as an ideal bridge between the validated and unvalidated Web."

Green, Samuel S. "Personal Relations between Librarians and Readers." *Library Journal* 1, nos. 2–3 (November 30, 1876): 74–81. A classic piece of library literature by one of the founding fathers of the American public library movement.

Houghton, Sarah. "Instant Messaging: Quick and Dirty Reference for Teens and Others." *Public Libraries* 44, no. 4 (2005): 192–93. An account of how the Marin County (CA) Free Library instituted instant messaging reference.

"Information Services Policy Manual: An Outline." *Reference Quarterly* 34, no. 2 (1994): 165–72. Provides a framework on which to build an information services policy manual.

"Invitation to Business Men." *Library Journal* 61, no. 21 (December 1, 1936): 911. The Pottsville Public Library advertises its telephone reference service to a particular clientele.

Janes, Joseph. *Introduction to Reference Work in the Digital Age*. New York: Neal-Schuman, 2003. A thoughtful look at the digital reference revolution by one of its leaders.

Jennerich, Elaine Z., and Edward T. Jennerich. *The Reference Interview as a Creative Art*. 2nd ed. Westport, CT: Libraries Unlimited, 1997. The reference interview as a "performance" requiring a particular set of skills.

Katz, Bill, ed. *Reference and Online Services Handbook: Guidelines, Policies, and Procedures for Libraries*. Vol. 2. New York: Neal-Schuman, 1986. Includes articles about the issues encountered in developing policy statements and reprints a number of reference collection and online policies in full.

Katz, Bill, and Anne Clifford, eds. *Reference and Online Services Handbook: Guidelines, Policies, and Procedures for Libraries*. Vol. 1. New York: Neal-Schuman, 1982. Discusses in detail the components of reference policies and procedures for academic and public libraries.

Katz, William A. *Introduction to Reference Work: Basic Information Services*. Vol. 1. 8th ed. New York: McGraw-Hill, 2002. The first volume of an often used and now somewhat dated textbook by the late reference expert.

———. *Introduction to Reference Work: Reference Services and Reference Processes*. Vol. 2. 8th ed. New York: McGraw-Hill, 2002. The second volume discusses reference services and techniques and includes an updated chapter on the Internet at www.mhhe.com/socscience/katz/.

Kern, M. Kathleen. *Virtual Reference Best Practices: Tailoring Services to Your Library*. Chicago: American Library Association, 2009. A concise handbook that outlines issues for consideration and provides sample plans and policies and much more.

Kister, Kenneth. *Kister's Best Dictionaries for Adults and Young People: A Comparative Guide.* Phoenix: Oryx, 1992. Although the reviews are dated, there is still value in Kister's discussions of the types of dictionaries and the field of lexicography.

———. *Kister's Best Encyclopedias: A Comparative Guide to General and Specialized Encyclopedias.* Phoenix: Oryx, 1994. The discussion of specialized encyclopedias and the basic principles of encyclopedia creation are still informative even if the actual reviews are dated.

Kovacs, Diane K. *The Virtual Reference Handbook: Interview and Information Delivery Techniques for the Chat and E-mail Environment.* New York: Neal-Schuman, 2007. A comprehensive handbook offering strategies for providing reference service in an online environment by an expert in the field.

Kuhlthau, Carol Collier. "Meeting the Information Needs of Children and Young Adults: Basing Library Media Programs on Developmental States." *Journal of Youth Services in Libraries* 2, no. 1 (1988): 51–57. Summarizes the developmental stages of young people in the context of library services.

Levine-Clark, Michael and Toni M. Carter, eds. *ALA Glossary of Library and Information Science.* Chicago: American Library Association, 2012. A guide to the terminology (and acronyms!) of library and information science.

Massey-Burzio, Virginia. "Education and Experience; or, The MLS Is Not Enough." *Reference Services Review* 19, no. 1 (1991): 72–74. Some observations on the importance of lifelong learning for reference librarians.

Measuring and Assessing Reference Services and Resources: A Guide. RUSA/RSS Evaluation of Reference and User Services Committee. www.ala.org/ala/mgrps/divs/rusa/sections/rss/. A guide to the literature of measuring and assessing reference services prepared by the RUSA/RSS Evaluation of Reference and User Services Committee.

Miller, Jonathan. "Quick and Easy Reference Evaluation: Gathering Users' and Providers' Perspectives." *Reference and User Services Quarterly* 47, no. 3 (2008): 218–22. Describes the method several Pittsburgh academic libraries used to evaluate the reference services they provide.

Naiman, Sandra. "The Unexamined Interview Is Not Worth Having." *Reference Librarian* 6, no. 16 (1987): 31–46. Reflections on what makes a good reference librarian.

Nolan, Christopher W. *Managing the Reference Collection.* Chicago: American Library Association, 1999. Provides guidelines on managing all aspects of the reference collection, including selection, evaluation, weeding, and more.

O'Gorman, Jack, ed. *Reference Sources for Small and Medium-Sized Libraries.* 7th ed. Chicago: American Library Association, 2008. Brief reviews of reference works intended "to serve as an authoritative buying guide for the purchase of reference collections for newly established libraries and for improving and expanding existing collections."

Patterson, Thomas H., John A. Damand, and Rachel Kubie. *Enoch Pratt Free Library Brief Guide to Reference Sources.* 10th ed. Baltimore, MD: The Library, 2000. A user-friendly handbook covering basic and popular reference works.

Pellack, Lorraine J. "First Impressions and Rethinking Restroom Questions." *Reference and User Services Quarterly* 49, no. 1 (2009): 4–6. Reminds us that *every* patron's question is important.

Radford, Marie L. "A Personal Choice: Reference Service Excellence." *Reference and User Services Quarterly* 48, no. 2 (2008): 110–15. An insightful, often inspirational editorial on excellence in reference service.

Radford, Marie L., and R. David Lankes, eds. *Reference Renaissance: Current and Future Trends.* New York: Neal-Schuman, 2010. A collection of essays based on the presentations given at the 2008 "Reference Renaissance: Current and Future Trends" conference.

Reference Services Manual. University of Massachusetts–Amherst. ERIC Document ED 200 211. The policy statement for reference service at the University of Massachusetts–Amherst.

Reitz, Joan M. *Dictionary for Library and Information Science.* Westport, CT: Libraries Unlimited, 2004. A comprehensive library lexicon that is also available online at http://lu.com/odlis/.

Rettig, James, ed. *Distinguished Classics of Reference Publishing.* Phoenix: Oryx, 1992. Signed essays tracing the history of thirty-one enduring reference works.

Riechel, Rosemarie. *Improving Telephone Information and Reference Services in Public Libraries.* New York: Neal-Schuman, 1987. Advice and suggestions for improving telephone reference service circa 1987.

Ronan, Jana Smith. *Chat Reference: A Guide to Live Virtual Reference Services.* Westport, CT: Libraries Unlimited, 2003. A comprehensive guide to virtual reference that includes practical advice and real-life case studies.

Ross, Catherine Sheldrick. "The Reference Interview: Why It Needs to Be Used in Every (Well, Almost Every) Reference Transaction." *Reference and User Services Quarterly* 43, no. 1 (2003): 38–43. A presentation from the RUSA President's Program at the 2002 ALA Annual Conference in which the author summarizes current research and offers her reflections on the reference interview.

Ross, Catherine Sheldrick, and Patricia Dewdney. "Negative Closure: Strategies and Counter-Strategies in the Reference Interview." *Reference and User Services Quarterly* 38, no. 2 (1998): 151–64. Analyzes the ways in which reference transactions are brought to an end.

Ross, Catherine Sheldrick, Kirsti Nilsen, and Marie L. Radford. *Conducting the Reference Interview: A How-to-Do-It Manual for Librarians.* New York: Neal-Schuman, 2009. Practical advice based on current research in communication theory, real-life examples, and helpful strategies abound in this comprehensive handbook.

Ross, Celia. "Keeping Up with Business Reference." *Journal of Business and Finance Librarianship* 13, no. 3 (2008): 363–70. Strategies for staying current in the practice of business librarianship.

Schmidt, Aaron, and Michael Stephens. "IM Me." *Library Journal* 130, no. 6 (April 1, 2005): 34–35. Promotes the use of instant messaging in reference service and describes some of its best practices.

Schneider, Karen G. "My Patron Wrote Me a Letter: The Joy of E-mail Reference." *American Libraries* 31, no. 1 (January 2000): 96. Encourages libraries to institute e-mail reference service and explains why they should do so.

Singer, Carol A. "Ready Reference Collections: A History." *Reference and User Services Quarterly* 49, no. 3 (2010): 253–64. Explores the history of ready reference collections and their transformation by electronic resources.

Smith, Sally Decker, and Roberta Johnson. "Reference Desk Realities." *Public Libraries* 46, no. 1 (2007): 69–73. A frank and funny look at what to expect when working at a public library reference desk.

Strong, Susan. "Sights, Sounds and Silence in Library Reference Service to Children." *Public Libraries* 43, no. 6 (2004): 313–14. Real-life examples and guidelines for reference service to children.

Thomas, Deborah A. "The Consumer Health Reference Interview." *Journal of Hospital Librarianship* 5, no. 2 (2005): 45–56. Addresses the challenges of providing health reference service and includes specific suggestions for the reference interview.

Tucker, James Cory. "Getting Down to Business: Library Staff Training." *Reference Services Review* 32, no. 3 (2004): 293–301. Describes the successful business reference training program developed at the University of Nevada-Las Vegas Libraries.

Tyckoson, David. "That Thing You Do." *Reference and User Services Quarterly* 47, no. 2 (2007): 111–13. Looks at the external demands placed on libraries and reference services and emphasizes the importance of serving the community's needs.

———. "What We Do: Reaffirming the Founding Principles of Reference Services." *Reference Librarian* 28, no. 59 (1997): 3–13. Examines Samuel S. Green's four principles of reference service and finds that they are still as important as they were in 1876.

———. "Wrong Questions, Wrong Answers: Behavioral vs. Factual Evaluation of Reference Services." *Reference Librarian* 17, no. 38 (1992): 151–73. Proposes a reference evaluation method based on behavioral factors and the accountability of reference librarians.

Vavrek, Bernard. "After the Guidelines and Reference Policy." In *Reference and Online Services Handbook: Guidelines, Policies, and Procedures for Libraries*, ed. Bill Katz and Anne Clifford, vol. 1, pp. 3–4. New York: Neal-Schuman, 1982. Emphasizes the importance of implementing guidelines for reference service.

Ward-Callaghan, Linda. "Children's Questions: Reference Interviews with the Young." *Reference Librarian* 2, no. 7/8 (1983): 55–65. An insightful look at the challenges faced by librarians providing reference service to children by one of the field's best.

West, Kathy, and Janet Williamson. "Wikipedia: Friend or Foe?" *Reference Services Review* 37, no. 3 (2009): 260–71. A report on a research study that evaluated the quality of a large and varied sample of *Wikipedia* articles.

Whitlach, Jo Bell. *Evaluating Reference Services: A Practical Guide*. Chicago: American Library Association, 2000. Practical methods, case studies, and an extensive literature review make up this comprehensive guide.

Wilkins, Craig. "Training Staff for Business Reference." *Journal of Library Administration* 29, no. 1 (2000): 37–45. Discusses the elements of effective business reference training and cites examples of training techniques.

WOREP, The Wisconsin Ohio Reference Evaluation Program. https://worep.library.kent.edu. Website of the reference evaluation program (WOREP) developed by Charles Bunge and Marjorie Murfin in 1983.

Yates, Rochelle. *A Librarian's Guide to Telephone Reference Service*. Hamden, CT: Library Professional Publications, 1986. A helpful albeit dated handbook on telephone reference service.

Zabel, Diane, ed. *Reference Reborn: Breathing New Life into Public Services Librarianship*. Santa Barbara, CA: Libraries Unlimited, 2011. Essays on current trends, developments, and challenges by some of the leaders in the fields of reference and public services librarianship.

LIST OF REFERENCE SOURCES
DISCUSSED IN PART 1

Acronyms, Initialisms and Abbreviations Dictionary. Farmington Hills, MI: Gale/Cengage Learning, 2001.

Alibris. www.alibris.com.

All Things Austen: An Encyclopedia of Austen's Works. 2 volumes. New York: Greenwood, 2005.

Almanac of Famous People. 9th edition. Farmington Hills, MI: Gale, 2007.

Amazon.com. www.amazon.com.

American Fact Finder. http://factfinder2.census.gov/faces/nav/jsf/pages/index.xhtml.

American Heritage Dictionary of the English Language. 4th edition. Boston: Houghton Mifflin, 2006.

The American Library Directory: A Classified List of Libraries in the United States and Canada, with Personnel and Statistical Data. Medford, NJ: Information Today, 1923–.

American Medical Association Concise Medical Encyclopedia. New York: Random House Information Group, 2006.

American National Biography. 24 volumes. New York: Oxford University Press, 1999. Supplements, 2000–.

American National Biography Online. www.anb.org.

America's Top-Rated Cities: A Statistical Handbook. Toronto, ON: Grey House, 2010.

America's Top-Rated Smaller Cities: A Statistical Handbook. Toronto, ON: Grey House, 2010.

Art Full Text. 1983–. New York: H. W. Wilson. www.ebscohost.com/wilson/.

Art Index Retrospective: 1929–1984. New York: H. W. Wilson. www.ebscohost.com/wilson/.

Association of Religion Data Archives. www.thearda.com.

Atlas of the World. 14th edition. New York: Oxford University Press, 2010.

Bartlett's Familiar Quotations. 17th edition. Boston: Little, Brown, 2002.

Baseball Almanac. www.baseball-almanac.com.

The Baseball Encyclopedia: The Complete and Definitive Record of Major League Baseball. 10th revised edition. New York: Macmillan, 1996.

Benet's Reader's Encyclopedia. 5th edition. New York: HarperCollins, 2008.

Biography and Genealogy Master Index. Farmington Hills, MI: Gale Cengage Learning. Online at www.galecengage.com.

Biography in Context. Farmington Hills, MI: Gale Cengage Learning. www.gale.com.

Biography Reference Bank. New York: H. W. Wilson. www.ebscohost.com/public/biography-reference-bank/.

Book Review Digest. New York: H. W. Wilson, 1905–.

Book Review Digest Retrospective: 1905–1982. New York: H. W. Wilson. www.ebscohost.com/wilson/.

Book Review Index Online Plus, 1965–. Farmington Hills, MI: Gale Cengage Learning. www.gale.com.

Books in Print. New York: R. R. Bowker.

Britannica Online. Chicago: Encyclopaedia Britannica. www.britannica.com.

Broadcasting and Cable Yearbook 2010. New York: R. R. Bowker, 2009.

Bureau of Justice Statistics. www.ojp.usdoj.gov/bjs/.

Bureau of Labor Statistics. www.bls.gov.

Business Rankings Annual. Detroit: Gale Cengage.

Business Statistics of the United States: Patterns of Economic Changes. 15th edition. Lanham, MD: Bernan, 2010.

Canada Post. www.canadapost.ca.

Canadian Almanac and Directory. Toronto, ON: Grey House, 2007–.

Cancer.gov: Statistics. www.cancer.gov/statistics/.

Chase's Calendar of Events 2011. New York: McGraw-Hill, 2010.

ChildStats.gov. www.childstats.gov.

Columbia Gazetteer of the World. 3 volumes. New York: Columbia University Press, 2008. Online at www.columbiagazetteer.org.

Compton's by Britannica. 26 volumes. Chicago: Encyclopaedia Britannica, 2010.

County Business Patterns. www.census.gov/prod/www/abs/cbptotal.html.

CRC Handbook of Chemistry and Physics: A Ready-Reference Book of Chemical and Physical Data. Boca Raton, FL: CRC, 1913–.

Dictionary of American Biography. 1927–1936. 20 volumes. New York: Scribner. Supplements 1944–1980.

Directories in Print. 32nd edition. 2 volumes. Farmington Hills, MI: Gale, 2010. Also available online as part of the Gale Directory Library.

Directory of Special Libraries and Information Centers. 38th edition. 3 volumes. Farmington Hills, MI: Gale, 2010. Also available online as part of the Gale Directory Library.

Education Full Text 1983–. New York: H. W. Wilson. www.ebscohost.com/wilson/.

Education Index Retrospective: 1929–1983. New York: H. W. Wilson. www.ebscohost.com/wilson/.

Education State Rankings: Pre-K–12 Education in the 50 United States. Washington, DC: CQ, 2010.

Election Statistics. http://clerk.house.gov/member_info/electionInfo/.

Emily Post's Etiquette. 18th edition. New York: HarperCollins, 2011. Online at www.emilypost.com.

Encyclopaedia Britannica. 32 volumes. Chicago: Encyclopaedia Britannica, 2010.

Encyclopaedia Judaica. 2nd edition. 22 volumes. Detroit: Macmillan Reference USA in association with Keter Publishing House, 2007.

Encyclopedia Americana. 30 volumes. Danbury, CT: Grolier, 2006.

Encyclopedia of Associations: International Organizations. 49th edition. 3 volumes. Farmington Hills, MI: Gale, 2010. Available online as part of the Gale Directory Library.

Encyclopedia of Associations: National Organizations of the U.S. 49th edition. 3 volumes. Farmington Hills, MI: Gale, 2010. Available online as part of the Gale Directory Library.

Encyclopedia of Associations: Regional, State and Local Organizations. 22nd edition. 5 volumes. Farmington Hills, MI: Gale, 2010. Available online as part of the Gale Directory Library.

The Encyclopedia of Chicago. Chicago: University of Chicago Press, 2004. Available online at www.encyclopedia.chicgohistory.org.

Encyclopedia of Hair. New York: Greenwood, 2006.

The Encyclopedia of Popular Music. 4th revised edition. 10 volumes. New York: Oxford University Press, 2006.

Encyclopedia of Southern Culture. Chapel Hill, NC: University of North Carolina Press, 1989.

Encyclopedia of Television. 2nd edition. 4 volumes. New York: Fitzroy Dearborn, 2004.

Encyclopedia of the Library of Congress: For Congress, the Nation and the World. Lanham, MD: Bernan, 2005.

Essay and General Literature Index. 1900–. New York: H. W. Wilson. www.ebscohost.com/wilson/.

Essay and General Literature Retrospective: 1900–1984. New York: H. W. Wilson. www.ebscohost.com/wilson/.

The Europa World of Learning. 61st edition. 2 volumes. London: Routledge, 2011.

Facts on File Encyclopedia of Word and Phrase Origins. 3rd edition. New York: Facts on File, 2004.

Famous First Facts: A Record of First Happenings, Discoveries and Inventions in American History. 6th edition. New York: H. W. Wilson, 2006.

FedStats. www.fedstats.gov.

Fodor's Travel Guides. www.fodors.com/guidebooks/.

Forbes Travel Guides (formerly *Mobil Travel Guides*). www.forbestravelguide.com.

Fulltext Sources Online. Medford, NJ: Information Today. www.fso-online.com.

Gale Directory of Publications and Broadcast Media. Farmington Hills, MI: Gale, 1990–. Available online as part of the Gale Directory Library.

Grolier Online. http://teacher.scholastic.com/products/grolier/.

Guide to Reference. 12th edition. Chicago: American Library Association. http://guidetoreference.org.

Guinness World Records. New York: Guinness World Records, 1956–.

Handbook of Denominations in the United States. 13th edition. Nashville, TN: Abingdon, 2010.

Handbook of U.S. Labor Statistics: Employment, Earnings, Prices, Productivity and Other Labor Data. Lanham, MD: Bernan, 1997–.

A Handbook to Literature. 10th edition. Upper Saddle River, NJ: Pearson/Prentice-Hall, 2006.

Historical Census Browser. http://fisher.lib.virginia.edu/collections/stats/histcensus/.

Historical Statistical Abstracts. www.census.gov/prod/www/abs/statab.html.

Historical Statistics of the United States: Earlier Times to the Present. 5 volumes. New York: Cambridge University Press, 2006. Online at http://hsus.cambridge.org.

Hoover's Handbook of American Business. Austin, TX: Hoover's Business, 2009.

Hoover's Handbook of Emerging Companies. Austin, TX: Hoover's Business, 2010.

Hoover's Handbook of Private Companies. Austin, TX: Hoover's Business, 2010.

Hoover's Handbook of World Business. Austin, TX: Hoover's Business, 2010.

Hoover's Master List of U.S. Companies. Austin, TX: Hoover's Business, 2010.

Injury Facts. Itasca, IL: National Safety Council. www.nsc.org.

Internet Library for Librarians. www.itcompany.com/inforetriever/.

ipl2: Information You Can Trust. www.ipl2.org.

The Library and Book Trade Almanac 2010 (formerly *The Bowker Annual*). 55th edition. Medford, NJ: Information Today, 2010.

Library Literature and Information Science Index. New York: H. W. Wilson. www.ebscohost.com/wilson/.

Marquis Who's Who on the Web. http://marquiswhoswho.com.

Merriam-Webster's Visual Dictionary. Springfield, MA: Merriam-Webster, 2006.

National Center for Health Statistics. www.cdc.gov/nchs/.

National Center for Health Statistics: Injury and Data Resources. www.cdc.gov/nchs/injury.htm.

The New Book of Knowledge. 21 volumes. Danbury, CT: Grolier, 2008.

New Century Cyclopedia of Names. 3 volumes. Englewood Cliffs, NJ: Prentice-Hall, 1954.

The New Food Lover's Companion. 4th edition. Hauppage, NY: Barron's Educational Series, 2007.

New Partridge Dictionary of Slang and Unconventional English. 2 volumes. New York: Routledge, 2005.

New York Times Index. 1913–. New York: New York Times Company. www.nyt.com.

No Shelf Required. www.libraries.wright.edu/noshelfrequired/.

Notable Last Facts: A Compendium of Endings, Conclusions, Terminations and Final Events through History. Haddonfield, NJ: Reference Desk, 2005.

The Old Farmer's Almanac. Dublin, NH: Yankee, 1792–. www.almanac.com.

OneAcross.com. www.oneacross.com.

Our Sunday Visitor's Catholic Almanac. Huntington, IN: Our Sunday Visitor, 1996–.

Oxford Atlas of the United States. 17th edition. New York: Oxford University Press, 2010.

Oxford Dictionary of American Quotations. 2nd edition. New York: Oxford University Press, 2005.

Oxford Dictionary of Modern Quotations. 2nd edition. New York: Oxford University Press, 2007.

Oxford Dictionary of Quotations. 7th edition. New York: Oxford University Press, 2009.

Oxford English Dictionary. 2nd edition. 20 volumes. New York: Oxford University Press, 1989. Also available online at www.oed.com.

Periodicals Archive Online. Ann Arbor, MI: ProQuest. www.proquest.com.

Periodicals Index Online. Ann Arbor, MI: ProQuest. www.proquest.com.

Perry Castañeda Library Map Collection. www.lib.utexas.edu/maps/.

Play Index. New York: H. W. Wilson. www.ebscohost.com/wilson/

Points of Reference. http://pointsofreference.booklistonline.com.

ProQuest Historical Newspapers. Ann Arbor, MI: ProQuest. www.proquest.com.

ProQuest Newsstand. 1977–. Ann Arbor, MI: ProQuest. www.proquest.com.

ProQuest Research Library. 1989–. Ann Arbor, MI: ProQuest. www.proquest.com.

Rand McNally Commercial Atlas and Marketing Guide. Chicago: Rand McNally, 1876–.

Random House Webster's Crossword Puzzle Dictionary. 4th edition. New York: Random House, 2006.

Random House Webster's Unabridged Dictionary. 2nd edition. New York: Random House Reference, 2001.

Readers' Guide Retrospective: 1890–1982. New York: H. W. Wilson. www.ebscohost.com/wilson/.

Readers' Guide to Periodical Literature. 1900–. New York: H. W. Wilson. www.ebscohost.com/wilson/.

Reference USA. www.referenceusa.com.

Reverse Acronyms, Initialisms and Abbreviations Dictionary. 3 volumes. Detroit: Gale, 2010.

The Rhyme Zone. www.rhymezone.com.

Rough Guides. www.roughguides.com.

The Scout Report. http://scout.wisc.edu/Reports/Scout Report/Current/.

Short Story Index. 1900–. New York: H. W. Wilson. www.ebscohost.com/wilson/.

Sports Illustrated Sports Almanac. New York: Sports Illustrated Books, 2003–.

The Statesman's Yearbook 2011: The Politics, Cultures and Economies of the World. 147th edition. London: Palgrave Macmillan, 2010.

Statistical Abstract of the United States. Washington, DC: U.S. Census Bureau, 1878–. Online at www.census.gov/compendia/statab/.

Subject Guide to Books in Print. New Providence, NJ: R. R. Bowker, 1957–.

Theatre World 2009–2010. 66th edition. New York: Applause Books, 2011.

The Time Almanac (formerly *Information Please Almanac*). Boston: Information Please, 1998–.

Toll-Free Phonebook USA: A Directory of Toll-Free Telephone Numbers for Businesses and Organizations Nationwide. Detroit: Omnigraphics, 2010.

Ulrich's International Periodicals Directory. New Providence, NJ: R. R. Bowker, 1932–. Also available online at www.ulrichsweb.com.

Ultimate Visual Dictionary. New York: Dorling Kindersley, 2007.

UN Data. http://data.un.org.

United States Census Bureau. www.census.gov.

United States Geological Survey. www.usgs.gov.

United States Postal Service. www.usps.gov.

Washington Information Directory 2010–2011. Washington, DC: CQ, 2010.

Webster's Third New International Dictionary of the English Language. Revised edition. Springfield, MA: Merriam-Webster, 2002. Also available online at http://unabridged .merriamwebster.com.

Whitaker's Almanac. London: A&C Black, 1868–.

Who Was Who in America, 1897–2010. 21 volumes. New Providence, NJ: Marquis Who's Who, 1942–2010. Also available online as part of Marquis Who's Who on the Web.

Who Was Who in America: Historical Volume, 1607–1896. Revised edition. Chicago: Marquis Who's Who, 1967.

Who's Who in America. 2 volumes. 65th edition. New Providence, NJ: Marquis Who's Who, 2010. Also available online as part of Marquis Who's Who on the Web.

Who's Who in the World. 28th edition. New Providence, NJ: Marquis Who's Who, 2010. Also available online as part of Marquis Who's Who on the Web.

Wikipedia. www.wikipedia.org.

Words to Rhyme With: A Rhyming Dictionary; Including a Primer of Prosody, a List of More Than 80,000 Words That Rhyme, a Glossary Defining 9,000 of the More Eccentric Rhyming Words, and a Variety of Exemplary Verse, One of Which Does Not Rhyme at All. 3rd edition. New York: Facts on File, 2006.

The World Almanac and Book of Facts 2011. New York: Infobase, 2010.

World Book Encyclopedia. 22 volumes. Chicago: World Book, 2010. www.worldbookonline .com.

World Health Report. www.who.int/whr/.

WorldCat. www.worldcat.org.

Worldmark Encyclopedia of the Nations. 12th edition. 5 volumes. Farmington Hills, MI: Gale, 2007. Also available as part of the Gale Virtual Reference Library.

Yearbook of American and Canadian Churches. Nashville, TN: Abingdon, 1915–.

INDEX